MIXED MESSAGES

Ann-Marie McMahon is a graduate of University College Dublin and a registered psychologist. She is Director of After-care at St John of God Hospital, Stillorgan, County Dublin, where her particular interests include counselling and psychotherapy.

She has a degree in Economics and Public Relations, and has worked in these related areas, as well as in personnel management.

She conducts courses in Personal Development, Human Relations and Communications for the Community and Adult Education Centre at St Patrick's College in Maynooth.

She has completed her Ph.D in Human Relations at Pacific Western University, LA, USA.

Ann-Marie's first book was the best selling *Issues, not Tissues: A fresh approach to personal development*, followed by *Bloom not Gloom: Self-awareness explored*. She is a contributor to the best selling *Stress File* as well as adviser to *Being You*. She is a regular contributor to newspapers, television and radio.

Sally McEllistrim is a journalist. She presents a news and current affairs programme with Carlow/Kildare Radio. She contributes news and feature articles to national newspapers.

Mixed Messages

Ann-Marie McMahon

with

Sally McEllistrim

ASHFIELD PRESS
DUBLIN

This book was typeset by
Gough Typesetting Services Dublin for
Ashfield Press,
26 Eustace Street, Dublin 2.

A catalogue record for this book is
available from the British Library.

ISBN 1 901658 00 7

All names and examples quoted in the text are fictitious.

Printed in Ireland by
ColourBooks, Dublin

Contents

PART III: THE COMFORTABLE SELF: DETECT – CONNECT – PROTECT

Introduction

The English language as spoken in Ireland must be one of the most charming languages anywhere. From the Kerryman jokes to dry Dublin wit, language and words play an important role of the Irish pysche. Sometimes, however, messages can be confused. It is not just the wit and humour that are mixed up and different, it is also the mixed messages that we carry through our daily lives. There can be an underlying confusion that seeps through the expressions that are commonplace, like:

- You look so well — I didn't recognise you
- You look so well now that you have lost the weight
- Isn't it a shame that you have no job after doing so well at school?
- They are such a nice couple it is a shame that they never had children
- She's great crack when she's drunk — she is totally different
- Who does she think she is?
- He is getting a bit big for his boots lately
- That pair seem to have forgotten where they come from
- I remember them when they were nobodies
- He is so attractive, how did he possibly marry her when all the gorgeous women in the town were after him
- She is so beautiful, I didn't expect her to be so good at her job
- He is a chip off the old block
- What good is a B.A. to you?
- He is a few sandwiches short of a picnic

All of these mixed and jumbled messages are all around us and they are taken for granted. It is no wonder that we can be so confused about things. Many of these messages can literally crush us and make us feel worthless. We can tell hilarious jokes, often at our own expense, but when we are low and vulnerable, the joke can misfire shake our self respect.

Mixed Messages attempts to look at the issues that come like a bolt out of the blue or sneak up on us unexpectedly in broad day light.

They come in the form of hidden agendas, assumptions, conflict, value systems, culture clashes, side kicks, put downs, verbal abuse, sarcastic notes, stranges vibes and angry tones.

Our beings can be literally sent swirling into orbit and feel as if we have been put through a spin dryer.

The confusion lying in our heads and on our bodies as a result of these missiles can lead us up a path of self-destructive and coping techniques that is not forwarded to our everyday vocabulary — shame, embarrassment, guilt, labels stigmas, wounds, alienation and shock.

These feelings can be steeped in further pain that leads us into shells that are so brittle that we never want to change.

Secrets and hiding become a way of life whether it be from the past — abuse, verbal, emotional or physical, or present — affairs, fraud, unplanned pregnancies, unemployment or death.

We find life difficult to cope with and we survive by pretending everything is alright. We put on a good show for the onlookers. We hope no one will suspect our inner turmoil or torment. We carry on regardless — often in a role alien to the self but pleasing to those around us.

Sometimes it can all get too much and the stress of sending confusing messages to keep up appearance takes its toll and has us on a road of addiction, strange behaviour, erratic thoughts and even suicide. The mixed messages may come from the person who has scant regard or thought for the poor and powerless but going to church service daily is paramount. It may come in the guise of the person so insecure and suffering with feelings of inadequacy that he/she has to try and belittle others and make them feel the pain also.

Mixed Messages tries to unravel the hidden self and will look at why we remain shackled in our pain, confusion and even instability. We look at why we nurse the pain instead of moving on.

To cope with what is around we need to detect what endeavour, connect to our real selves from further threats to our dignity and sensitivities. It is only through the process of looking under the covers that you will be able to reveal your own strengths.

In an age when messages are being conveyed to us daily be it from newspapers, T.V., radio, E-Mail or Internet we need to support and protect ourselves from futher mishaps.

For some the confused messages have lasted too long, perhaps steeped in tradition with no real foundation. They can leave us confused and blurred by themysteries of cultures, trends, fashions and labels.

When we finally learn to make some sense of the messages bombarded by parents, teachers, relatives, friends, neighbours, employees, politicians, clergy we can interpret what is really being said and what our reactions to these messages.

We will now know about what is on the inside and we can try to deal with the blows.

Parents should, from an early age, try to clarify the messages they hand to their children rather than "Don't do as I do, do as I say".

Children learn from examples. They learn from body language. They listen, not only to words, tones and untonations. They decipher the message from the various cliches, cultural sounds, codes whether it be a child in Hong Kong, Tehran or Dublin. They are all the same — learning to grow and they perceive the message as they literally see and hear it. They imitate practice and belief what their parents do. The beauty of the child is in his/her innocence, spontaneity, naiveity and totally willingness to practice the message from the parents. Let's not spoil or ruin the next generation. If you have received the wrong message, correct it and give someone else a break.

Acknowledgment

This book could not have been written without the enthusiasm, energy, insight and journalistic skill of Sally McEllistrim. Thank you Sally for turning an arduous task into a positive and enjoyable experience.

I also want to thank Alan Kennedy for his wonderful cover design displaying artistic skills par excellence. Thanks also to Aidan Culhane for editing together with Gilbert Gough for his speedy typesetting. Colour Books rounded it all off with their superb printing.

Finally, thanks to my publisher, Gerard O'Connor, for taking another risk and I hope this book brings dividends to all our wonderful readers.

In memory of my late Mother

PART I:

THE HIDDEN SELF: THE PARTS WE DON'T REVEAL

1. The Self

The Continuous Journey of Self-Discovery

Do you like yourself? It might seem like a thought-provoking question but for many, what you don't like about yourself would seem like a much easier question to answer. Most of us could rattle on about our shortcomings — our fat thighs, big nose, small eyes, shyness, feelings of insecurity and lack of skills, etc. This is an image of ourselves which we carry inside us. Very often we live our lives according to this self-image. In other words, the person who considers theirself as a failure can indeed often fail in the same way that a person who considers theirself a victim will find circumstances to justify this. This image is often the base on what your entire being, including your personality and behaviour are built.

John fails miserably in his exams. Instead of realising that he did not study hard enough, he thinks, "Oh well, I've proved my parents right, they never believed that I could do anything well". The important thing to realise is that your self-image can be changed, for the better, but only when you come to realise what your inner voice is saying to you. Self-assurance only comes when you recognise your own voice. Very often, a negative self-image can be akin to a bad habit. You have become used to its damaging and dangerous messages. Instead, try to get used to the positive messages that your voice can also send you.

You are unique. Allow yourself to feel your uniqueness. Let us take some examples of people who have become trapped in their own bad self-image, people who are looking on at life from the sidelines. They envy those for whom life is a constant, exciting and changing picture. They are fearful of taking up any challenge, no matter how small, for fear that they will never be able to achieve any success. People say:

- I'd love that job, but I'd never be able for it; or

- I'd love to go on that holiday, but I've nobody to go with; or

- I'd love to go to college and do a degree but I am too old; or

- I'd love to leave my job but I have to keep up with the mortgage; or

- I'd love to get married but who would want me?

In all these examples there is one common denominator — poor self-image and because your self-image is so negative it has become a life-long partner to you. You are shackled by its familiarity. But you have the choice to break its hold on you and be free to live a happier life.

Awareness of self comes when you are prepared to throw off the chains of negativity and start a journey of self-discovery which will include self-acceptance, self-actualisation and self-realisation. When you start to become aware, you go through a process. Perhaps your moods begin to change according to the issues that you are confronting. Try not to be too critical. It will be difficult initially but the rewards are tenfold. You will be freer and lighter, relieved of the awful load of self-doubt and negative self-image and not weighed down by fear and pain. Concentrate on what you do even though you are nervous. For example, "I know that I want to make new friends; although I'm nervous I'm going to make as much effort as possible and I am not going to let the nerves stand in my way of finding fulfilment." Perhaps even learn to notice what is going on for you. What is actually happening to you when you do something different? Do you enjoy yourself? At first, it will probably be very difficult to look at yourself and the issues that are preventing you from living life to the full.

People who are perfectionists, for instance, may find it very difficult to recognise that they are seeking an unrealistic sense of perfection for themselves and others. For some it may be necessary to create a new self-image in their head through the process of visualisation. They may have to start visualising a self that is going to be confident and able to cope in lots of different situations. In other words, you have to get a better mental picture of yourself. People who go for plastic surgery very often want a new face. Before they get the job done they have a chat with the doctor whom they trust to perform the operation. They then discuss what they want, telling the doctor about their expectations of the operation and hope the outcome will be beneficial.

For many of us, professional help is a luxury that we cannot afford. What we can do is help ourselves by visualising the way we really would like to be. Initially, it may be difficult to see yourself, as this confident, secure person. Do not be afraid to seek the help of your friends. Talk your problems over with them and get their support. This is a vision of the new you. Your aim is to become more self-assured, self-confident and stronger. At the beginning there may be a strong element of fear and risk, because for so long your lack of confidence and self-worth was the shadow that haunted you. But what you must remember is that the only risk you are taking is a positive one on the path to better self-esteem and security. In the pursuit of a new self, you will also encounter the pursuit of meaning which will give you a choice of direction.

The dangers that you may encounter include people who might feel threatened and hostile to the changes in you. For so long you may have been a very passive person willing to fit in with the demands of others, but suddenly you have learned a new word "NO" and the first time that you say "no" to someone you may feel uncomfortable with their reaction. People will get used to you asserting your self and try as you might you can never change how somebody else reacts but you can change how you react. With the wonderful gains, you may also have losses. You may lose the friends who are insecure about the changes in you but if they cannot accept the positive side to you, keep the memories of your friendship and move on.

Perhaps in order to achieve your goal you will have to go through a process of self-detachment, looking at yourself from the outside — often with a sense of humour at what you see.

Humour can be an extraordinary weapon in pursuing your new image. Avoid going down the road of self-pity or self-rejection. Habits such as self-pity and resentment go along with an inferior self-image. Basically, you picture yourself as a victim and somebody who does not deserve happiness. Even in your new journey of discovery, there will be days when you will automatically think back to those negative thoughts. Remember however, that your resentments are not caused by other people, events or circumstances but by your own emotional responses. You can have power over this if you convince yourself that your resentment and self-pity are not ways to happiness and success, but instead are pitfalls. Self-pity does not fit in with your new mental picture of yourself. It is a negative feeling and serves only to ensure failure.

When you are in the role of the victim, you are giving somebody else power over you and this minimises your own power. A feeling of emptiness can also be a symptom of an image of inadequacy so it is important that you work hard to rid yourself of this feeling at all times. It is also important to look at the negative indicators to avoid the ruination of self. When you are driving a car and you see the flashing light notifying you that oil is needed, you would automatically pull in at a petrol station and fill up.

Your body also gives you signals. Listen when it tells you that you are tired or stressed. Take time out to relax and rejuvenate yourself. When you eventually become self-assured you will recognise that as well as being confident, you will also want to be competent and have belief in yourself. The belief that we can utilise our resources to produce and regulate events in our lives should be non-threatening. We must realise that while we will make mistakes along the way, we will withstand them and learn to cope with uncertainties and challenges that test our capabilities. People with a sense of high self-efficacy approach a task in a very different way to those with low self-efficacy. They are never shaken by changes. They take them in their stride, even enjoy them and they are never overwhelmed by a sense of failure. They don't allow themselves to feel threatened and they persevere even when the going gets tough.

We are living in a culture where people are being constantly bombarded with the need for self-improvement and the struggle for perfection. The images of rich, successful, intelligent, good looking people are being presented to us as ideal role models. We can feel threatened if we don't live up to society's code of what is acceptable. We are terrified of being made to feel stupid and looking like losers. Once we attain a feeling of quiet self-assurance we can accept the success of others. We can recognise our own achievements and value our own worthwhile contributions. There is a wonderful sense of contentment when we appreciate and see our own attainments.

Sometimes it does take courage to embark on this journey of self-improvement. We will be challenged within ourselves and forced to look often at our secret selves. Part One of this book will be looking at the inner pains that we encounter while Part Two looks at issues and skills. Finally Part Three looks at the supports that we need to become more self-confident, self-assured and capable of displaying or revealing our true selves to deal with the cards life send us.

Consider Annie who is living alone in a tiny flat. She has many friends but she rarely invites them to her home as she is ashamed of her small surroundings. She feels that her friends, most of whom live in expensive houses, would somehow look down on her and criticise her for not owning her own house and for putting up with living in such a dingy area. She pretends to them that she rents two flats in the house. She is living a lie which is putting pressure on her. Inside, she knows the reality — she knows that she is fooling her friends because of her lack of confidence. She is afraid to open up and does not believe that they would accept her for living in different circumstances to them. In fact she is not giving them credit for accepting and liking her for what and not who she is.

Mary always appears immaculate. She is always turned out in the best clothes, with beautiful accessories and perfect make-up. People around her feel very ill at ease because they cannot live up to her standards. Mary however is disguising the fact that her parents have emotionally neglected her. She does not articulate this but instead presents an image that she thinks is acceptable to the world around her. The reality is that she has created a fence around herself to hide the emotional turmoil within.

Steven has a very successful career. Living up to this, he drives a top-of-the-range BMW. He has a wide circle of friends who have not attained as much material success as he has, but he sees himself differently. He comes from a working class background and as a young child he always envied people who were well off as he saw them as powerful and valuable. As an adult he measures himself and others in the same way and he does not believe that he is worthwhile without being able to show off the material trappings he has accrued. The material wealth only fills a small part of Steven's psyche.

Sometimes we are so overwhelmed by feelings that we are as if we have two selves. We feel in conflict no matter what we do or what we feel. It is like we have a divided self and mixed messages ripple through our lives. The aim of this book is to unravel some of those inner voices, which perhaps have given rise to torment, turmoil and have tantalised some of us to amazing lengths. *Mixed Messages* aims to clear up some of the messages created by misunderstandings, hidden agendas, verbal war weapons, exhausted taboos, shame or skeletons in the closet and leave you with a better sense of self, better dignity, better respect and above all to feel supported, and secure in your self.

Very often how we judge people may affect how we behave towards them.

Roisin has beautiful blonde hair and a very pretty face and some people think that she is just another dumb blonde. Patrick is a comedian but some people think that he should keep the jokes coming even when the show is over. Mandy is a single mother and some men think that she sleeps around. Joan goes to mass every day so some people think that she is a wonderful person. Hilary is a great sport — very funny and always game for a laugh. Some people do not acknowledge that she has a very demanding job as they think that anybody who is that much fun cannot be responsible. Audrey always uses big words — so some people automatically think that she is marvellously intelligent.

No matter what vibes we give out we all have to ultimately live with ourselves. Life is too short for turmoil and pain that can be eliminated once we understand what messages we are sending and receiving to ourselves and others. We deserve to feel good, not once "in a blue moon", but on a daily basis to help us cope with what life sends us. The following chapters will be you toolkit towards creating a more comfortable you. Good luck and enjoy a good read.

2. Shame, Embarrassment and Guilt

Experience and effects explored

You say something out of place in a work or social situation. Those around you react with embarrassment, and perhaps even hostility. You cringe with the awful feeling of shame and humiliation and feel as if everybody in the room is looking at you and thinking that you are stupid. You feel so ashamed of yourself and wish that you could go away and bury your head in shame. "Bury your head in shame" is just another of the cliches that we bandy around as if we were experts on moral and social behaviour. They form part of our everyday vocabulary. Though these words can be thrown out thoughtlessly, they can have severe and long lasting effects on the people they are aimed at. Can you imagine what it must be like to carry feelings of shame with you throughout your life? Those who do, experience feelings ranging from total devastation to isolation or exclusion. There can be often mixed messages of excitement and desire. However, these last two reactions may not be always apparent.

How can shame be exciting? Well, if you do something in a moment of exhilaration but reflect on it with embarrassment, for instance getting drunk and behaving irresponsibly either sexually or socially, then the excitement that you felt can be tinged with shame. The same can be said of desire. You may desire something or somebody but feel ashamed of those feelings. You may perhaps have feelings for somebody who is married and you might be guilty and ashamed of those desires. You may be looking after an elderly parent and silently wish that you had more time for yourself to do the things that you want to do. These feelings can, subsequently, throw up very strong feelings of guilt. How could you possibly want to leave your elderly parent who has done so much for you? Perceived feelings of selfishness can provoke feelings of guilt. Think of a child who is unfettered by the awful ties of shame. The child is spontaneous, full of zeal and open to the world. Think then of an adult burdened by shame. For him or her, spontaneity and zeal can result in shame. To avoid that painful feeling the adult controls it and ends up living a life devoid of energy, fun, excitement and unlike the child, is closed to the experience of living life in a free and happy way.

The basic question that must be asked is "why do we feel ashamed?" When do we first experience shame? Very often it can be as a result of an experience in childhood. A child can be getting used to his or her sexuality and does not understand that it may not always be appropriate to run around naked. Perhaps its parents are giving a party and the child suddenly appears in all its glory. Some parents can handle a situation like this very well. They can treat it with the humour that it deserves and gently explain to the child that nakedness is natural, It's not to be frowned on but that there are times that it is just not acceptable. On the other hand there are parents who do respond rather differently. Because of their own feelings of embarrassment they chide the little child with cutting words like, "you should be ashamed of yourself", "you dirty little thing". Now that child has two issues to deal with. He or she is upset at the reaction to its nudity and added to that is the sting of the words. The child feels dirty and from then on will associate being naked with being dirty. This can have a severe and long lasting effect and will carry through to other areas of its life. He or she may experience difficulties sexually, emotionally or socially in later life.

Let us take the scenario of the child who decides to respond to this put-down by lashing out and creating an angry scene. This leads to a power struggle between parent and child and culminates in the parent slapping the child. Now there is physical as well as emotional pain. The memory of the physical pain may be clear but the shame of being put down is not so it is buried (it is often easier to bury what is not understood). This has much more serious consequences. It can create the perfect background for the feeling to be recreated, often without realising why. It can create a susceptibility to feeling ashamed, often with out any tangible reason — the seed has been planted. Words are like weapons. They can be directed to wound, even unwittingly but for long after they are spoken, the feelings they have evoked can be felt like a harsh slap and they can leave painful memories imprinted on our minds.

Basically shame arises when our self-respect is somehow under attack and in a way we may feel that we want to go under cover. The following are typical examples of persons whose dignity has been compromised and attacked.

Anthony is dyslexic. His parents and teachers were not aware of this when he was going to school and his lack of progress was put down to laziness and lack of intelligence. He was regularly singled out for unfavourable attention by his teachers who held him up as an example to his fellow classmates as being weak and slow. His work declined even more. He was alienated by his classmates and he bore the brunt of his parent's dissatisfaction with him. This lack of understanding by his parents and lack of professionalism by his teachers was very damaging to Anthony. Now in his thirties, he has never quite overcome this attack on his self as a young child. He is racked with shame when he makes mistakes in work or even when out with friends and the thought of having to read something out loud in public fills him with terror. With a little more foresight by his parents and teachers, Anthony's difficulties as a young child could have been recognised and he would not have to dread being held up as an example of ridicule.

Being different from others can create feelings of insecurity and vulnerability in children who thrive on wanting to fit in and to feel that their families are more or less the same as everybody else. Rachel's family had very little money when she was growing up. Everything was a struggle for her parents — buying school uniforms or books and paying for school outings, Christmas or birthdays. Try as they could they never managed to keep up and Rachel always felt that she was looked down upon by her fellow classmates whose parents were better off than she. She often felt excluded from the excitement and fun of school outings as her parents could only afford to send her on a rare occasion.

Rachel is now married with children of her own. She has succeeded in making a good life for herself but she has never succeeded in shaking off the pain of being put down, and feeling as if she and her family were not good enough. As a result she over compensates by splashing out large amounts of money on clothes and jewellery for herself and ensures that her children and husband are beautifully turned out. She has courted people with money as her friends. Because of her deep-seated shame and insecurity, she places undue emphasis on the value of money and sadly, she has passed this on to her children. Rachel is typical of someone who has felt the pain of exclusion and is shamed by this.

Children can also feel left out if their parents are different to others, for example if they are older or less glamorous, if their jobs are not as high profile or respected or indeed even if their parents live in a way that is unusual or contrary to the norm. If criticism is directed at a child's parents, the child feels this just as much as if it was aimed at him or her.

Let us take the example of Gerard's parents who were both alcoholics. When he was growing up his happiness and security was upset by rows, angry scenes and the complete uncertainty at what was going to happen next. It was not uncommon for him to be woken in the middle of the night by his mother, who was drunk herself, and berating Gerard's father for his behaviour. Other nights' sleep was broken by dreadful screaming and shouting and his mother's threats to leave the house, with Gerard and his two little sisters. Added to this was the awful shame of bringing friends back to his home as he was always fearful of what condition his parents would be in. Almost all of his birthday parties were destroyed by the terrible tension created by his parents' drinking. He was deeply ashamed of how they acted when drunk and he was very conscious of the fact that his friends were looking at his parents through eyes that were distrustful and sometimes even disrespectful.

Gerard now lives with the pain and insecurity associated

with his parents drinking. He burns with shame when he thinks of the times that he had to follow them into pubs in the hopes of persuading them to come home and he will forever remember the hostility of people who watched them stagger home. Shame is often like a deep wound and it can be opened up again with painful and shameful memories.

David and his brother and sister were orphaned when they were young children. They went to live with their father's sister and husband who had no children of her own. Both paid special attention to David's siblings while never having much time for him. This feeling of isolation was compounded by the children's other relations who also sang the praises of David's brother and sister and generally ignored him. They were boosted up and made to feel loved and cherished. He was brought down and made to feel unloved and unwanted. Because of this shame he invented parents who loved, wanted and were proud of him. He revelled in this fantasy world and often his fantasies spilled over to his daily life and he would pretend to strangers that his parents were alive. It was David's way of coping with his parents' deaths.

David's sense of shame was now being felt on two levels. He was deeply ashamed of not receiving his aunt's and uncle's love and he was also ashamed of being an orphan. His siblings did not feel this shame as they were cherished. He on the other hand was not and associated orphans with a Dickensian image, which was in a way a reality for him.

Shame can be felt on many different levels because of so many different experiences. In the long run it can create feelings of shyness, embarrassment, anxiety, guilt and humiliation. Shame can also be handed down from generation to generation and its harmful effects can be mirrored in those to whom it has been handed down. Elderly people can often attempt to pass down their tradition of shame to their relatives. Take for example the young pretty girl who is heading out on a date. She has taken great pains with her appearance and feels that she looks terrific. Her elderly grandmother however is not so impressed with her dress as she feels that it is too short and might give people the wrong impression. She says this to her granddaughter, who takes offence at her remarks and a blazing row follows with the grandmother saying that she looks disgraceful and will attract unwelcome attention. The girl answers that she couldn't give a toss about what others think, with the grandmother retorting that she must cater for the minds of others.

This is a perfect example of how shame that can be passed on. The grandmother is caught up with the need to fit in and conform to the expectations of others. She has grown up with the need for approval and she has always been ashamed to be different in case this would result in being relegated to the fringes. On the other hand her granddaughter is unburdened by this shame and insecurity, but the reproach has been felt and if this were to continue, it would undoubtedly result in the girl questioning her own individuality and feeling that she is to blame for the negative reactions of others. She would sub- sequently inherit the trap of shame.

There is very little that is positive about shame. It creates emotional pain that leaves the person with deep seated feelings of torment, vulnerability, introspection and humiliation. The person who is saddled with shame and guilt is often convinced that he or she is damaged, defective and different. These feel- ings of powerlessness can create a vicious circle. The person feels that he or she is worthless and does not have the right of self expression. As a result he or she cannot share these feelings with a trusted and understanding friend and essentially contin- ues to be locked into a world of dark shame.

Examples of how persons can be ashamed to talk about their feelings of shame are typified by victims of rape, incest or abuse. Patricia was raped when she was 19. She had gone on holidays to Italy to celebrate passing her college exams. Though her parents were concerned at first about her plans to go on her own, she managed to convince them that she was well able to fend for herself. During her first week in Italy she met up with a group of English speaking people and became particularly friendly with a young man and they often broke away from the others and did their own thing. He was attractive, intelligent, fun and attentive and Patricia enjoyed his company and trusted him. This trust was shattered when he raped her one night.

Patricia is now 45. She is nervous and insecure and ever since the rape she has been battling with feelings of guilt and shame. She feels guilty of trusting a person so easily who was capable of violating that trust. She feels guilty that she didn't heed her parents advice and go with a friend. She feels guilty that perhaps her behaviour contributed in some way to what happened. She feels terribly ashamed of the rape, so much so that she has never told anybody about her ordeal. It has only been through counselling that the subject has been broached. To others it may seem that Patrician's guilt and shame are misdirected and misplaced. To her they are part of what she is. This example indicates how both guilt and shame can be interlinked.

Shame can sometimes act as a protective mechanism, for example in cases of incest where the feelings of shame can go hand and hand with protectiveness. Niamh suffered systematic abuse at the hands of her father as a small child. Her memories of childhood are clouded by recollections of dreading her bedroom door opening at night and the feeling of being weighed down with confusion, hurt and degradation. Her father's repeated assertions that she was a bad girl and that the abuse was a special punishment served only to increase her feelings of shame and guilt. She grew up with the feeling that she deserved the abuse. Further to this, she has also been conscious of how abusers are perceived in society as well as being ashamed of herself. She is also deeply ashamed of her father and thinks of him as a sick pervert. Not telling anybody has been her way of protecting him. Sadly her behaviour as an adult has been ordained by her childhood experiences.

There is a strong overlap between shame and guilt. Sometimes guilt can serve as a defence against shame. Guilt is associated with wrongdoing which we can try to rectify. There is also the added possibility of forgiveness. Not so with shame. Shame can be seen as a weakness and is not always easily recognised as the ashamed person does not feel that he or she has permission to talk about it. Sometimes they cannot even bring themselves to acknowledge its existence.

Our sexuality can also be tied up in such a way that it can be linked to shame. Sex is powerful and natural and is part of us. But it is one of the areas most often associated with shame and guilt. Poor body image, lack of confidence or self-esteem and the feeling that one is undeserved of love and care can all inhibit and starve our ability to lead full lives.

Let us take the example of Angela who is 33. She is very attractive, bright and full of fun but she lacks self-esteem and is very self conscious. She was deserted by her father when she was a tiny child and as a result she has come up against a lot of problems with men. Deep down she doesn't really believe that any man could in any way ever love her. She feels very unsure in the company of men and this can translate into flirting and feeling nervous when going on dates. She dreads meeting a new man and feels embarrassed if one shows her affection when in public as she feels that people will be looking on and thinking that she is not good enough for him. Equally she can sometimes think that he is not good enough for her and this leads her to be ashamed of him. Basically this is a double bind — she doesn't think that she deserves a man's love and she is ashamed of this.

There are also very strong mixed messages associated with the beginning of puberty. The young boy who experiences wet dreams can very often misunderstand these and this can lead to him feeling ashamed of his dreams as if they were unclean.

The old tradition of Catholic women being churched in Ireland following the birth of a baby raised very strong feelings of shame and guilt. A lot of women felt that this was to cleanse them of dirt following sexual intercourse and they felt shamed and guilty because of this. In turn some even resented their babies which subsequently led to feelings of guilt.

Marriage is still seen by many as the ideal state and in the main it is still seen as bringing fulfilment, happiness, togetherness and love into people's lives. But the people who are not married can often be ashamed of their single state as they feel they have to account for this and explain why they are unattached. It may seem that in this day and age being unmarried should not be a cause for shame but many people feel driven to invent partners as the pain of admitting that they don't have anybody special in their lives can be too much too bear. Some even stop going to social occasions as they don't feel strong enough to withstand what they imagine to be other people's pity and questions.

Shame and guilt can also be attached to extra-marital affairs. Earlier we touched on shame being connected with desire and excitement — things that are done in a frisson of excitement and desire. Affairs can be the same. There is always the initial excitement, fun, desire, passion, intrigue and tension attached to an affair — a roller coaster of feelings. The married party can be afraid that their spouse will find out and they can burn with the feelings of shame that this would bring. But this fear is rarely strong enough for them to stop the affair. Though they may feel guilty about deceiving their partner they can revel in the excitement that the other person has brought into their lives and they feel both guilty and ashamed that they are not strong enough to give their lover up. They are also caught up in a web of lies and deceit and can feel ashamed that they are weak and lack the character to stay faithful to the person that they originally married.

Gary got married to Ruth when they were both in their early thirties. They have three lovely children, good jobs, a comfortable lifestyle and they enjoy the respect and affection of both their families and friends. To the world they appear happy and contented. Gary however has been having an affair for the last four years with a woman that he met while away on business in another country. This woman represents, for him, the calmness, serenity and quietness that is totally lacking in his marriage and that is very important to him. He comes from a background that was very disruptive to his sense of security. His father drank heavily and he and his sisters cowered in fear, together with their mother, in anticipation of one of his regular outbursts. He always felt guilty that as a young child he couldn't protect his mother from his father's anger and watched helplessly as blows rained down on her from his drunken father.

This filled him with guilt as he felt he should be able to do something to make his father stop. He went on to marry a woman who also came from a broken home who is fragile and vulnerable emotionally but also given to extremes of temperament. In fact this was one of the things that he noticed about her when they first met, her mood swings were recognisable to him. But though familiar, he still longs for peace and the other woman fills this need. However, he does love his wife and he is riddled with guilt when his wife confronts him. He also feels terribly ashamed because he doesn't have the strength to finish with his lover and he perceives himself as weak.

Pauline's affair was brief and lasted for just a few months but it turned her life and that of her family upside-down. Her husband was kind and loving and devoted to their little boy. All of her friends liked him and told her that she was so lucky to be married to such a nice guy. But for her that was part of the problem. She often actually resented her husband because he was so nice. She felt that he was boring. One night she met another man at a party. It wasn't a case of love at first sight, more a case of lust at first sight. Though she never grew to love or really respect her lover, she enjoyed the passion and excitement that they shared. When eventually her husband found out about her affair he was devastated. She will never forget the hurt, the pain, the disillusionment and the disappointment in his face when he confronted her and shortly afterwards he left her. She is deeply ashamed that she could disregard the solid qualities he had in favour of somebody who had little else but a good looking face and a sense of fun. She also feels terribly guilty that her son will now grow up without two loving parents who are together and she feels that she has deprived him of this security. Basically Pauline is feeling ashamed firstly of herself and feels that she has let herself down by not having a good value system. She feels that she has let her husband and child down for a few moments of passion.

Anticipated shame can often be a protective measure and can be just as damaging. It prevents the person from leading a full and active life as he or she is so terrified of failure and the shame this would involve and so lives life in a safe and non- challenging way. The person avoids situations that are likely to cause shame, thus opting out, and constantly plays down his or her expectations and those of others. For instance John is plagued with feelings of anticipated shame and will tell people that he couldn't possibly apply for the job, take part in the race or act in the play as he wouldn't be able for the challenges. The variations are endless but the theme, or the reasons for this are the same. The person has lessened the expectations of others and feels that if other people don't expect much, they cannot be disappointed. The shamed person is then saved the embarrassment of their scorn or indeed pity. This is a protective mechanism. This in turn leads to a merry go round as the fear of being exposed to shame creates feelings of shyness and feelings of shyness produce shame. Often, rather than dealing with these feelings the person creates other feelings, akin to anxiety.

Anxiety is like fear and the constant fear of failure can hinder the individual in so many ways. Many may dread going to work in the morning, dread going on a date or even dread walking in to a room alone. There are also fears of entering into relationships, be they with potential partners or friends as this poses a risk of being abandoned and rejected. Shame can affect us by tying us down. It limits our freedom and we become self-conscious and stilted. The physical actions accompanying shame can be likened to a person shrinking in some way. It can be a very intense emotion akin to feeling under attack.

Joanna who is 31 is terrified of going to public places on her own. To the world she appears confident and assured but inside she is constantly in a knot of worry and suffers badly from sensations of anticipated shame. She feels that the eyes of everybody will be on her if she enters a restaurant or pub alone. She is terrified that people will criticise her looks, dress or even the very fact that she is alone. On the occasions that she has to go to places on her own she is very self-conscious and suffers from the imagined rebuffs of others. She genuinely believes that others are talking about her in a disapproving way. As Joanna is so ashamed of herself she constantly expects the censure of others, even strangers.

This constant fear of criticism can sometimes lead people to become easy targets for those who can sense their insecurity. It can mean that the person becomes dependent on the very people who will use this against them. They are so afraid of being rejected that they become people-pleasers, always eager to please and behave accordingly.

There is a very important distinction to be made between shame and embarrassment. Embarrassment is an emotion that passes soon after the episode that created it. Certainly it is an uncomfortable feeling at the time but shame is related to something that is much deeper and can also be linked to what we will deal with in later chapters, secrets and labels. The transience of embarrassment can be summed up by the following example.

You are at a dinner party and the hosts have gone to great lengths to ensure that everything is perfect for their guests' enjoyment. The party is swinging and everybody is in jovial form. Suddenly you lean over to chat with another guest and in the process you knock over one of the crystal wine glasses. There is a small silence and you cringe with embarrassment. You apologise to your hosts and offer to replace the glass. The feelings of embarrassment are very strong and very real, but essentially they are fleeting and don't remain forever. In time you will be able to recall this moment with mild feelings of embarrassment and maybe even turn it around to make it a funny story at another time.

After reading about the damaging effects of shame you may possibly wonder, how on earth can shame ever be appropriate. Well shame can exercise certain functions. It can sensitise us to the sensitivity of others. It is the little inner voice that warns us that we may be attacking the dignity of another human being.

For example it is what prevents us from drawing attention to another persons shortcomings and subjecting them to feelings of humiliation. At a more personal level it stops us from leaving the house suitably non-attired for a social or personal engagement. It is the feeling of having to adapt to certain norms in society that protect an individuals sense of power. In certain cultures it acts as a deterrent for crime as people would be so ashamed of bringing disgrace on themselves and their families. In Japan it is not uncommon for people at a theatre for instance to leave their personal belongings at their seats and go and use the lavatory, secure in the knowledge that other Japanese people would not steal them.

Kiss-and-tell stories, where people sell information about the lives of celebrities or those in the public eye can create untold grief, hurt and sadness, for those whose lives are the subject of the publicity. This is a double edged sword. Often the thing that stops people from revealing sordid stories is the shame that would result in this action. "Has he or she got no shame?" would be the accusation that the person would have to deal with.

Remember that you can not only cope with shame, but you can rid yourself of its harmful and limiting effects. Look at where it is evident in your life. Look at how it is holding you back. Look at how it affects you. Look at the thoughts that go with your emotions of shame, fear, dread, disgrace, mortification, worry and anxiety. Look at the reality of your situation. It is important to examine why you feel ashamed. Ask yourself what are you ashamed of. Try to get a clear picture and understanding of this. Ask yourself is there something that I can do to make this situation better. Look at the areas that you can let go of. For example if you are suffering with shame that has been transferred to you then realise that you are living in a different era, in different circumstances and with very different social, cultural and moral values.

Bear in mind that not so long ago it was considered the ultimate disgrace for somebody to have a baby out of marriage. People were even ashamed to go to mass without wearing a hat or to be seen arriving late. Things are different today. The process can be likened to putting all the pieces of a jigsaw together. Initially you may think that there are too many pieces and that you will never make sense of it all, but little by little it will become clear. Think of the people who will be on your side and only too willing to help you. With professional counselling and help you will be given the security of exploring all the things that cause you shame and ultimately you will be able to free yourself from their ties.

Changed circumstances can sometimes result in people feeling humiliated and lost. For those who were used to being in secure and lucrative employment, with enviable lifestyles, any fall from this can lead to very strong feelings of shame. People feel that they have to try to put on a good face for their friends and business acquaintances and this can be very pressurising.

Deirdre and Michael had always enjoyed a very high standard of living. Both had come from what is popularly known as "moneyed backgrounds" and lived life in a whirl of social and professional engagements. Through a combination of misjudged business deals and a stock market collapse they ended up bankrupt. The difference in their lifestyle left them very insecure and fearful for the future. They were conscious that their friends pitied them and they felt that they had to constantly reaffirm the fact that they had always been used to having money and position. They feel deeply ashamed of their new found poverty and see their status as 'being diminished' in the eyes of their peers. Both feel very stressed and under pressure with the veil of secrecy that is surrounding their lifestyle.

Another example of shame is when you are ashamed of your own body.

Paula is very overweight. She has had to endure the insults, rejection and disdain of people who think nothing of asking her when is she going to go on a diet or do something about her weight. She has had to go through the stares and jeers of strangers in the street who point her out and laugh with their friends. Going out to pubs, restaurants and night-clubs is a nightmare for her as she is conscious that her friends will be chatted up and asked to dance and that she will be left on her own in a corner. It has now come to the stage that she hates going out and as a result she stays at home and eats more to compensate. She feels desperately ashamed of her weight and often feels very angry at the thoughtlessness and lack of consideration shown to her as a result of how she looks. The harder she tries to diet the more she eats and life becomes a vicious circle.

Isolation becomes her companion and eventually friends give up on her. Her shame becomes so deep that she loses all self-respect. The shame in fact almost leaves her without energy to get up and do anything about herself. It is not until she reaches rock bottom and hospitalisation faces her that she starts to turn the wheels for recovery. While the initial plan is to lose the weight, it is the long-term plan of looking at the shameful image that will free Paula from the chains of her own pain.

There are so many areas in a person's life that can give rise to him or her feeling ashamed. Some women, particularly those who are unmarried or without a long term partner can be very ashamed of feeling that they would like a have a child. They can convince themselves and others they do not want to have children as they feel that any acknowledgement of this would leave them vulnerable and open to the pity of those who may see their single state as less than whole. On the other hand there are those who feel that the pressure put on them by society to have children places a burden on them. These people can equally feel ashamed if they do not want to have children, because society values parenthood and those who do not wish to have children for whatever reason are often perceived as bring selfish.

Bernie is 29 and married. She has a busy career life and she does not want children. Her husband and parents however see her as being selfish and hard and in heated arguments with her husband he often accuses her of being selfish and even irresponsible. He does want children and he makes Bernie feel ashamed of her lack of desire to have a baby because of his constant demands on her and his affirmations that she is disregarding his needs.

Marcella's child Darina committed suicide eight years ago. Since that day Marcella has been haunted by memories of her daughter and tortured with feelings of shame, embarrassment and guilt. Both sad and happy memories mingle in her mind. She experienced terrible feelings of shame following Darina's death, particularly when she is in the company of new people who might innocently or unwittingly question her domestic situation of family life. This shame inside her evokes feelings of anger. Marcella feels angry with people's questions but only because she is so terribly ashamed that her child could commit suicide. So the vicious circle continues. Marcella was brought up in a deeply religious family who always felt that suicide was one of the ultimate sins. She feels that Darina let both her family and her faith down and this embarrasses her greatly and them predictably Marcella feels awfully guilty about these feelings. She believes that she should have realised Darina's intent and done something to help her daughter. Then there is the double bind. She believes too that by feeling ashamed of the circumstances following her daughter's death, she is actually ashamed of her daughter.

Ruairí is thirty four. When discussing death and dying he tells people that his father was killed in a sailing accident. However, he committed suicide by drowning. Ruairí was about five and in the years that have elapsed he has always yearned for normality. Suicide was always a taboo subject for his family and his father's death was always spoken about in hushed tones. As a result Ruairí has always associated his father with shame and felt he was a symbol of shame. He has never properly grieved for his dad and as such the memories are alive and stirring. Memories of shame, isolation, darkness and guilt haunt him regularly. When the parents of Ruairí's friend, Jonathan, dies he has almost envied him his openess to grieve. He feels that he has a right to be sad and a right to talk about his parent's death.

Suicide can leave a trail of shameful and guilty feelings felt by those left behind.

Remember you don't have to live with the feelings of shame, embarrassment or guilt for the rest of your life. Learn to understand where the feelings are coming from and protect yourself.

Going to the grave with these feelings was done generations ago. Today with awareness, knowledge and information we can learn to cope and deal with shame in a more appropriate manner. It is never too late to change the way you feel. Be patient and persist. The longer you postpone your decision the more time you allow the feeling to fester. Give yourself a break. Seek help now and free yourself from the shackles of destructive emotions. Don't leave it too late.

3. Labels and stigmas

Your false image

Did you ever find yourself in a situation when somebody said something to you that you felt was completely at variance with how you saw or felt about yourself. You may have been called a flirt, a snob, mean, an alcoholic or even stupid. You may have been described as coming from a rough background, as being bad tempered or lazy. You may have even been introduced as being somebody's wife, somebody's daughter or somebody's employee. In other words you were labelled.

Stupid, lazy, mean, crazy, neurotic, hypocritical are just some of the labels we pin on individuals without ever really stopping to think about how these will affect the people they are pinned to. Labelling a person can demean him or her and threaten their individuality. They are often judged solely by their label, not as a person with so many different qualities and so many different rights and needs.

The label becomes all important. People who sit in judgement generally don't waste much time in trying to seek out what's beneath the label. Its often much easier to accept the label even if it has been unjustly attributed to somebody. It saves trying to get to know the person and unfortunately we are living in a society where time is a precious commodity. Consider the following example. You are having some friends round for dinner and you're running late as you were unavoidably held up at work. You run in to a supermarket to pick up a few things that you have forgotten. You dash to the freezer section and look at the ice creams on offer. You recognise some of the brands and decide that they will do. This has saved you the trouble of having to look further and you can go on and enjoy your evening.

It is fair to say that sometimes our dealings with other people are conducted in this same way — safe, fast and with out much thought or effort. Naturally some labels are important, but our exploration of others and ourselves is a continuous process and we should try never to leave a person feeling short-changed. What is normal? Most people perhaps would have a different definition of what is or what is not normal. For some normality could mean going to work each morning, going on a holiday once a year, meeting friends for a social occasion, getting married, having children, enjoying a drink in the company of others. It could even be owning a house, a car, a video, a television, having a bank or building society account.

However for other people normality could mean not having any of these things. They may be perfectly happy not owning a television or a house, not getting married, not having children. This is normal for them. What is normal for some is different for others. Conforming to the conventions of others may not be some people's idea of what is right or good for them. For instance some people are looked on as being weird or odd if they prefer their own company to that of others. But for some people it is perfectly acceptable and they are happy and contented in their own company. They don't feel as if they have to fit in with other people's standards and routines.

Generally anyone who steps outside the status quo is considered a bit "odd" or "strange" and sometimes people feel unsure in the company of those for whom normality is "different". Its important to note that abnormality is only what the majority of people regard as such. Social attitude is very often the creator of many labels that in turn can create enormous anxiety.

Peter is married to Alice who is divorced. They grew up together and always got on well. When they finished school, Alice left Ireland and went to work abroad and they lost contact for a while. She married and later divorced. Eventually she decided to return and she and Peter met up again at a village reunion. They felt totally at ease in each other's company and began to meet on a regular basis. They were aware of the growing attraction between them. They felt rather uncomfortable with this as they were worried of how their relationship would be viewed by others, particularly the other members of their family who were extremely conservative. They made several attempts to end their liaison but they were in love and finally decided to do what was right for them and what made them happy. They told their relations, who as they suspected reacted with alarm. Peter's mother made it very clear that she saw their relationship as wrong. She maintains that Alice is still married to someone else. She and other family members refused to go to their wedding. This hurt Alice and Peter very deeply as they feel that they have done nothing but love each other. They have been labelled and stigmatised by their relationship and all because some people just cannot accept that love sometimes does not have boundaries.

People who are from different races and colours are often subject to much hostility simply because they are different. It does seem odd that white people seem to think that they are better or supreme, especially when one considers the obsession that they have to get a tan. In fact white people can be all different shades throughout their lives. They can be blue when born, red when they are sunburnt, purple when they're cold, pink when they are embarrassed. We can turn white with anger, yellow when we are sick. All these colours, yet we are so quick to point the finger elsewhere. Sometimes we need to look at our own labels before we start attaching them to others.

When you think of the term "stigma" what images does it present? Automatically you could perhaps think of people who have been tainted by life events — those who have served time in prison, been in a psychiatric hospital, been sacked from their jobs, unemployed or people from a social class that is not desirable. But why do we stigmatise others so readily? Why do we presume that we have the right to make judgements on other peoples lives or circumstances?

Originally the term stigma originated in Greece where it was used to describe the visible sign that slaves were marked with. The Christian term "stigmata" means outward wounds that indicate an inner grace or worthiness. In Nazi Germany the Jews were marked with a number to signify their religion. In other countries people who have been in prison carry a mark which identifies this. It is important to note that what is considered abnormal or strange behaviour in one culture may be acceptable in another. In Muslim countries it is normal for the women to dress in clothes that cover their heads. In eastern culture it is normal for monks to shave their heads and don long robes. In western culture it is acceptable for people to dress in clothes that are less constrictive.

There is still a great deal of stigma attached to mental illness. People who suffer or have suffered with mental illness are seen by some as disturbed or unstable. "Odd", "not right", "a half wit" and "not the full shilling" are just some of the expressions that are used to describe a person suffering with mental disorders. These are cruel, ignorant and thoughtless accusations. The whole study of Psychiatry and Psychology has evolved so much that many believe that it is very difficult to define who is or not "normal". The real problem with labelling someone abnormal is that it can cause very real and serious traumatic consequences for that individual. It can go on to cause them much personal, professional and social difficulties. It can prevent them from moving forward and more seriously it can lead to them experiencing discrimination when seeking a job or applying for a permit to work in another country.

When people are labelled, others can have negative expectations of them. Take the case of a boy whose teachers are told that he is different. The teachers then go on to treat him in the very way that encourages him or her to be different. When a person is classified as different or abnormal all of his or her actions or behaviour patterns are judged in this light.

Alan served five years in prison for his part in an armed robbery. He used his sentence to study computers and became very interested in sociology. During this time he reflected on his life of crime and resolved that when he left prison he would try to lead a more useful and constructive lifestyle. When he completed his sentence he began looking for work but he was unsuccessful. When potential employers learned of his prison record they were unwilling to give him a chance. He feels angry and frustrated by this and fears that he will carry the stigma of his prison record for the rest of his life.

In a world where material success is considered so desirable, unemployment can also create a lot of stigma for people. Paul has been unemployed for the last eight years. Initially he believed that he would eventually find another job but he has long since despaired of ever working again. He is conscious that some people think of him as a "dosser", "a scrounger" or incapable. These are some of the labels that are directed at unemployed people. He feels very uncomfortable and sometimes humiliated when strangers ask him what he does for a living. He believes that in a world where huge emphasis is placed on a person's social status, his unemployment renders him somewhat lesser socially and he feels stigmatised by this. There is also stigma attached to people marrying those who are considered to be from a different background — "he isn't her type", "he married beneath him" are some of the comments cruelly hurled about.

Sarah comes from what would be considered a privileged background. Her parents are wealthy and she was brought up in a style that reflected this. She fell in love with Derek who was brought up in different circumstances. His parents had very little money and did not have the benefits of education. Sarah places very little importance on a person's social standing. However her parents and friends were aghast when the couple announced their plans to get married. They saw Derek as being totally "beneath" Sarah and couldn't understand why she wanted to marry him. In fact her parents felt that she was letting them down and her friends didn't want to be in any way associated with Derek's circle.

In the last chapter we spoke of the difference between shame and embarrassment and the fleeting nature of embarrassment. Stigma can be felt as deeply as shame and often labels can be quite superficial, like embarrassment. They can be changed, but stigma is much deeper and it sticks. Certainly a label can sting, but a stigma wounds. Just think about all the stigmas that are attached to a person's lifestyle. If a woman works or has worked as a prostitute she is automatically called a whore, a tramp or a slut. The fact that she may change the direction of her life does little to affect the stigma that has been created by her past. If a person is homosexual he has to bear the stigma that surrounds his sexuality. Stigmas go very deep and even though thoughts and attitudes are changing it is very difficult for some people to openly express their sexuality as the stigma in relation to homosexuality is still apparent.

Liam is gay. He has no difficulty with his sexuality and feels very comfortable in the company of his friends who are very supportive. He believes that he has met the person with whom he wants to spend the rest of his life and they are very happy and committed to each other. It pains him then when he has to endure the scorn and innuendo of passing acquaintances who feel that he is a target for their prejudice and abuse. He gets very angry and frustrated about this and sees the stigma surrounding homosexuality as causing very real pain and torment for himself or his friends. Though Liam is happy and has come to terms with his homosexuality, he still experiences the outrage of ignorant people who are not comfortable with any person who is outside what is considered to be the norm. Many homosexuals are trapped within marriages that they entered into as a cover for their homosexuality. Others hide in relationships with heterosexual people while some experience desolation and resentment as they feel that their sexuality is open to condemnation and prejudice.

Hilary is 38. She is attractive, intelligent, fun-loving and gay. Only her closest friends know this. To her parents, relatives, work colleagues and acquaintances, she has been unlucky in love and has resigned herself to the single life. For Hilary it is easier to allow them to think this, though she often resents the smugness and self righteousness of her family and friends When they refer to gay people, she doesn't feel that they could ever understand or accept her lesbianism. She often feels guilty that she isn't strong enough to be open about her sexuality and feels that she is living a lie. Though she is tired of fending off questions about whether or nor there is a man in her life, or when she is going to settle down and have children, she believes that this is a small price to pay to avoid the stigma of being a lesbian.

George is 32. He lives in a rural area with his elderly parents. He is desperately lonely and has attempted suicide on a number of occasions. He cannot communicate his feelings with anybody as he fears that it will get back to his parents. He feels trapped in two ways. Firstly he feels trapped in the stigma surrounding homosexuality and secondly he actually feels trapped in his own homosexuality. He often wishes that he was heterosexual and able to express love, care and affection for a woman.

Geraldine is married. She is 34. She realised that she was a lesbian in her early twenties, but tried hard to repress her feelings. She believed that she wouldn't be able to cope with the negative attitudes of people. When she met Mark, who was kind, caring and madly in love with her as well as being totally unaware that she was a lesbian, she decided to accept his proposal of marriage. She saw this as her way of fitting in and being accepted in society. Also she believed that she could learn to find emotional and sexual fulfilment with a man. This however was not to be and she began to resent her husband and bitterly regret her marriage to him. She felt jealous of her other lesbian friends who were unshackled by the need to be accepted by others. The marriage ended which proved to be very traumatic for both herself and Mark. He felt used and disgusted that his wife could physically love another woman. She feels guilty that she has put Mark through this traumatic time.

The sad realisation is that labels stick and sometimes the individuals who put them there are not even aware of the damage they have caused. At the end of the day it is important to be true to yourself and comfortable in your own body. If a label stings, do something about it. Challenge the person who attempts to belittle you or talk through your situation with a friend or professional person to make life more comfortable for you. Above all learn to be content in your own skin.

4. Scars and inner wounds

Does this world hurt you?

Picture a little boy who falls and cuts his knee. The child is stunned and shocked by this and when he sees blood he begins to cry and looks around for help. His parent soothes him and puts a bandage on the cut. Eventually with some tenderness and care, he begins to feel better. When the bandage is removed, there may initially be a scar, but in time this fades and the young boy forgets all about the experience. His parent ensured that he was properly cared for and nature healed the pain. The child was comforted, protected and perhaps learned that sometimes its better to walk rather than run. In adult life we can ask the question do we find it is as simple to heal our emotional wounds. The general answer is in the negative as we are often so unsure of the area that has been hurt. We do not always recognise emotional hurts as easily as physical ones.

Emotional scars come in the form of the self being hurt and this can leave us wounded, raw or scarred. These scars prevent us from being fulfilled. We are unable to open up to others and can end up being over-sensitive and bruising easily. Take for example the little boy who constantly bumps into things because he is not looking where he is going. He ends up with bruises. Likewise the hurt adult ends up with a personality that is wide open to bumping into situations and experiences that seal its hurt. We can end up feeling alone — as if there is no one to administer the care and love that is so vital to happiness and security.

Consider, for instance, Gillian who was left with a deep ache when her boyfriend Henry left her. Her situation was all the more painful as not only did he leave for the other side of the world, he left with another woman and subsequently married her. Gillian's hurt centres on her feelings of betrayal by Henry.

She feels let down, cheated, vulnerable and insecure. She even feels that he has taken her good memories of their time together and stood on them. She is eaten up with feelings of jealousy for his wife which is ultimately destructive for her. She feels that she will never be able to trust another man and subsequently has vowed that she will never get involved with anyone again.

This is the scar that Gillian lives with. She is experiencing life with the barriers that she has erected. Her self-esteem has plummeted and she even rejects the help that friends offer her. Her emotional scar is now so deeply ingrained that others cannot see it and she has become isolated. People are tiring of trying to get through to her and think that she is happy with her life of isolation and alienation. Some people on the other hand do not have such deep scars but are constantly prone to feeling slighted. Again the hurt may not go very deep but the constant feelings of being insulted, looked down upon and feeling left out can make them very vulnerable that puts a dent in their competency. Many of the rebuffs they feel are imagined as they are constantly on the alert for put downs. Eventually they become super-sensitive and thus the scars go deeper.

Bríd has always suffered from feelings of inadequacy and she always thinks that others are gossiping about her and feeling that she is not really good enough. People have become used to the fact that she is always on the defensive. Some seem to be accustomed to this and so she has become an easy target. On the occasions that she tries to assert herself and take them up on something that they have said which has offended her, she is told that she is too sensitive and that nobody can say anything to her. When people say this to Bríd she immediately regrets that she has tried to stand up for herself. She thinks that the others are right and she tries then to make them accept her. She essentially becomes a people-pleaser ever open to the whims of others. She does not feel strong enough to withstand the rejection of others, and the imagined rejections that she has felt in the past often become self prophetic. People who feel the pain of inner scars and wounds can often turn to substances which they feel will lessen the pain and they try to loose themselves in drink, tranquillisers, cigarettes or food. The pain however does not go away and the person may then have to deal with feelings of lack of willpower and eventually may end up with serious addiction problems.

There are so many reasons why a person carries the pain of inner wounds. He or she may have been subjected to much hurt and pain and the resulting wounds were never tended to or given the opportunity to heal. Wounds like shame can be passed on to other people. They can bear the burden of other people's hurt and this can even become a poison that can affect a whole family. Separated people, for example, can often feel cheated and saddened by their separation. They can harbour very strong feelings of resentment for their partner and then this poison can have a ripple effect on the family. It can pass on to their children and to many other areas of their lives.

Cathal is 43. He experienced much trauma and turmoil as a young child due to his parents' marital difficulties. They were locked in a cold unloving union and as such vented their anger and frustration on each other and on the children. In particular Cathal's father would criticise his wife regularly and pull the child into confidences that he was much too young to keep or to understand. Cathal felt very confused internally at being the confident and as a result was scared emotionally due to this constant confusion.

People who carry grudges can be people who carry scars. We are all familiar with the saying that someone "has a chip on his/her shoulder". It may be truer to say that this person has a scar on their shoulder. They have never been able to let go of past hurts and they have never been able to get over them. People who feel the need to bully others, be it in the school, work or social environment feel very threatened by the security of others. They resent the fact that others do not suffer with the pain that they carry and they are constantly seeking out victims. They believe that somebody is always out to get them. Examples of these feelings can be typified in the parent who bullies his or her child. Strangely instead of appreciating that the child is having a scar-free life they may resent the child this freedom and set out to control or limit them.

Equally there are people who nourish their hurt and scars too much and as a result fall into the role of victim or the "poor me syndrome". This excuses them from taking on responsibility and gives other people the power to reaffirm what they feel are their weaknesses. For some , their past hurts may serve as an excuse to opt out of situations. This is understandable. If somebody is constantly told that they are flawed they can hold on to this, and believe it. If a child is told that he or she is stupid, the slightest mistake that he or she may make in later life will be seen as a confirmation of this.

It is natural that when you make a mistake you can be shaken or a little dented by that experience but a mistake is just that — a mistake. Do not turn your mistakes into a big crisis. Learn from them. If possible, try to rectify them. Equally, somebody's harsh words, though very hurtful and painful, are just words and should not be constantly replayed in your memory. This just reinforces the hurt and stops you from moving on. As with minor mistakes, you don't have to carry hurt with you and you can heal the minor wounds. The deeper ones are certainly more difficult to deal with.

Catherine received notice to go for a medical for a new insurance policy. Not a regular visitor to doctors Catherine felt very anxious on the day. Aged 38 she is slightly overweight and she was hoping that the doctor would find nothing major wrong with her. As the doctor looked at her throat he commented on her crowned teeth in a put-down manner. Testing her blood pressure he commented on small scar on her arm joking her about trying to "burn herself". Finally on coming to her weight he said "for a middle aged woman you could do with getting rid of the pounds". While nothing dramatic happened and no major problems were detected Catherine felt very hurt at the mixed messages that were hurled her way. While the doctor meant no harm, Catherine was sensitive and the comments went very deep and she left the surgery feeling very bad about herself. She came away feeling very put-down and her emotions were scarred more deeply than the insignificant scar on her arm.

Grudges, resentments and pain require much work. Think of them in terms of requiring emotional surgery. Give yourself the time to recuperate. An important part of the healing process is forgiveness. To go forward you must try and learn to forgive the person who has hurt or wronged you. It is not easy, but it is vital for you and the freedom that it gives you. Freedom from feelings of anger, revenge and resentment makes it all worth while. When you carry these feelings, you are eaten up by them and can even go on to cause other people pain and they in turn continue to beat themselves. Even physical appearance mirrors how you feel inside. You can look weighed down, twisted and bitter. Think then of the person who has come to terms with the emotional scars that they have been carrying. They have decided that these emotions have no place in their lives any more and they try to have them removed. It is strange when you think of the amount of time, energy and importance that we give to our physical appearance, with scant regard for our emotional well-being.

If a person is unhappy with his or her physical looks he or she goes about changing them in some way. It could be losing weight, changing their hairstyle or updating their clothes. A lot of thought and planning usually goes into these changes. The same thought and planning should be taken by the person intent on ridding him or herself of emotional scars and pain. It is a gradual process, but the rewards are great. The important thing to realise is that the scars can be healed and there is much help available today via counselling, therapy and self-help groups.

Therapies can include:

Psychoanalysis — the goal of this therapy is to make the unconscious conscious. This is done through dream analysis and free association of thoughts while the patient lies on a couch or otherwise relaxes. It is a prolonged form of therapy which can take several years to complete. The restructuring of the personality is more the aim than the solving of immediate problems.

Family and marital therapy — this form of therapy focuses on the personal dynamics between the couple and/or the members of the family. It concentrates on bringing to the surface conflicts between the individuals and finding ways of resolving issues that create disharmony.

Cognitive-behavioural therapy — this focuses on the explicit behaviour of the individual and his or her thinking processes. The aim of the therapy is to correct inappropriate ways of thinking and therefore to allow the client to behave in new, more personally adaptive ways.

Humanistic therapy — this focuses on the present interpretation of problematic events from the past. The client learns to understand better how and why he or she has reached a certain impasse in their life and how to move forward from it.

Constructivist therapy — this focuses on the different aspects of each individual personality and how they can come into conflict with each other and with other individuals. Its aim is to help the client understand how to integrate different personality characteristics better and thus how to lead his or her life in a more aware and controlled manner.

5. You and your shadow

Discover your other side

Did you ever notice that on a sunny day you can see your shadow. It almost feels as if there is another person walking beside you. It stays with you, it belongs to you, accompanies you. The shadow only emerges on a sunny day. For some reason, nature keeps our shadow hidden on darker days. It's almost that we are happy to show ourselves when the sun is shining and that and we want to show ourselves off to the world. During the darker times, the shadow fails to appear as if it is hidden in the dark recesses of our beings. It is like the part of us that we don't want to reveal. Imagine a big willow tree, its luxurious leaves and branches cast a long shadow over the surrounding grass. Equally a shadow can often be cast over our personalities. Sometimes we can even feel uncomfortable about our shadow. The psychologist, Carl Jung summed it up when he said that the shadow is the thing that a person has no wish to be. For many of us the shadow is the darker side that seems to surfaces at unexpected moments.

We all like to display the lighter and brighter side of our personality but our shadow side can often peep through. This is most obvious in our relationships with other people. We can often behave irrationally, be bad tempered, moody, jealous and the like. This can be our shadow side battling to walk beside us. Sometimes we are not in touch with our shadow and we end up projecting it onto somebody else. Basically we can condemn others for their weaknesses without ever really examining our own weakness, our own shadow side. Our relationships with others, particularly during times of unease or adverse relationships can force us to confront our shadow selves.

Relationships are all about being connected to other people and they come in various guises. We have social and casual relationships. We form relationships with those whom we work with and with those we live near. In fact we have so many different forms of relationships, friendship, kinship, pen-pals, platonic friends, best friends, intimate lovers, family and marriage partners. There is a lovely old Irish saying, "it is in the shadow of others that we live" — we need other people. Though we may be independent and able to get on with things ourselves, we are generally happiest when we are in relationships with other people, when we are loved, needed, respected and cared about. By our very nature we are social animals and we thrive on contact. Some relationships, however, are quite puzzling. They can cause us pain, sadness and grief and quite often they force us to confront our shadow side. We may be born and die alone, but in between we need to reach out and be connected with our fellow beings. We seek to reaffirm our existence by reaching out and making contact with others. People strive to enhance each other and discover their own identity through giving, receiving and sharing. But we are human and imperfect and often our striving for perfection for ourselves and for others can leave us feeling let down, short-changed, resentful and inadequate. It may be reality and it can be a cold experience for some. Perfect relationships are as much an illusion as perfect love. Relationships involve trying to confront and manage our own vulnerabilities and anxieties as best we can.

There is a strong link between relationships, health and happiness. Forming a new relationship that we believe will help bring us contentment and fulfilment is one of life's joys but losing a relationship is one of the worst experiences. It can leave us feeling sad, depressed, lost and abandoned. Good relationships mean that a person has support, is happier and usually has good mental, emotional and physical health. The most stressful event in a person's life is losing a relationship, be it through death, divorce or ending a partnership. Research shows that susceptibility to illness is greater among those who are widowed and divorced. The loss of a close relationship is one of the main causes of depression. When we are depressed, sad or lonely our shadow can lurk beside us and our positive, happy and bright sides can be overshadowed. We all bring a personal history to our relationships which also includes our shadow. As well as bringing our capacity to think and feel, our sense of worth, our anxieties, our sense of wonder, our sexuality and expectations we also bring our darker sides.

Sam has a wife, two children and a good job. However this does not seem to keep him happy or satisfy him. He is envious of others who he considers better off. It is like a shadow side settling on his shoulders saying "do better do better". As a result of this nagging feeling, he never stops to appreciate what he has, but rather constantly plays the part of the begrudger. His work suffers due to his insecurity and he is constantly rowing with his wife, who finds it difficult to understand him. In fact, Sam is living in the shadow of his father who died at a young age. He subsequently felt he always had to do better to make up for his father's early death.

To avoid the shadow side being exposed people often erect barriers to hide their real selves and to create a self that they feel is acceptable to others. Many consciously set out to do this, while others do so subconsciously. These barriers can prevent us from reaching out to others and from growing in any way. Our defences are there to protect us from possible hurt. A person may find it difficult to express a deep emotion so they disguise it with another less threatening one. An example of this can be the person who is seething with anger and resentment and does not want to put their anger on display so he or she adopts "a couldn't care less attitude" which is very effective at keeping others at arm's length. Jealousy is an emotion that we are all good at disguising. People often use sarcasm and caustic wit to hide their jealous side. Projecting blame onto others is another barrier, but what we often project is our shadow self. Criticising others is a tool that takes the spotlight off ourselves. People are very good at pretending or putting on the best possible faces, the outward show.

As children we entered the magical world of make-believe. "Let's pretend" was the cue to visit an often enchanted world where possibilities were only limited by our imagination. In adult life, pretending can be an escape from reality. We can conceal our shadow side and pretend that the face that we have chosen to show is the real us. There is nothing wrong, of course, with keeping certain things private or keeping things to ourselves. It is only when we pretend to be something or somebody that we are not, using pretence as a means of avoiding reality, that problems can arise. We can become caught up in a web of lies and deception. We can pretend to like things or people that we cannot stand, but inevitably our shadow side rises to the surface and we can then be seen as two-faced. A lot of these games come into play between couples. A woman can pretend to like her mother-in- law to please her husband. Friends can pretend to like doing things or going places to go along with their friends' wishes. People can attend various church services to pretend that they are adhering to the dictates of the church. Men and women can play hard to get, pretending that they are not interested in getting together and as a result they often lose out on the chance of forming a loving and lasting relationship. People can pretend that they are enjoying a better standard of living that they actually do. There are so many masks for so many different situations. This can put extraordinary pressure on those who live in the world of pretence.

In our dealings with others there is a huge capacity for manipulation, game playing, misunderstanding, jealousy, resentment and obsession. Our emotions, if not balanced can play upheaval for both us and those with whom we are involved. When games or manipulation are being played out, there is very often a hidden agenda — a mixed message. The hidden agenda may be the shadow side of the person re-appearing and causing ruffles in what might otherwise have been a good relationship. The shadow is often seen in obsessive relationships. Individuals sometimes find themselves in unhappy and destructive relationships that can border on addiction.

Many will identify with obsessive relationships akin to fatal attraction. Obsessive relationships often distract from reality. You are trying to live out the shadow side of you that has been asleep for so long. The relationship becomes almost like a witch-hunt for you. Your partner is a crutch for you and is constantly on your mind. You fail to enjoy doing anything without the presence of this person. In fact, the person becomes like an object you could put on a pedestal. You refuse to believe anything which paints a less than glowing picture. Obsessional love includes following the person around, finding out things about them which they are not ready to divulge and then trying to use the information directly or indirectly to keep the person tied to you. You can't leave the person alone. You think nothing of phoning the person ten or more times a day and you would call around out of the blue for no particular reason, regardless of the other's feelings.

An obsessed person can do desperate things in a desperate attempt to, perhaps, live out a shadow side. Sadly the recipient can get badly stung and can be very confused by your behaviour. Very often, the obsessed person fails to look at the problem in their own life.

Shadows can lurk in the dark in the shape of the former self. Take for example Beth, aged 16 and wanting desperately to be like her friend Liz who is chased by all the boys. Beth is two stone overweight. When she decides to diet, she is full of enthusiasm and loses the first stone quite easily. She struggles with the second stone but eventually shifts not two stone but five stone. Basically her former heavy self is gone and she almost feels naked, but sadly the diet has gone into overdrive and she cannot stop. Dieting is controlling Beth rather than the other way round. When she eventually loses six stone, she knows she is in trouble and longs for the old shadow, the weight that once protected her from society.

Basically, over compensating is a symptom of other areas in a person's life that are not being dealt with. The woman who is involved with the violent alcoholic who saps her self-esteem but who continues to enable and support him to treat her so badly may be addicted to his bad behaviour. Her shadow side may be stronger that the part that wants to break free and live her life. She may be obsessed with wanting to change him and get him to respect and value her. The woman who is aware of her husband's infidelities, but continues to turn a blind eye may be somebody who is addicted to being a victim. The woman who becomes involved with a married man, with the full knowledge that he is never going to leave his wife may be addicted to him, obsessed by him and her shadow side may be the side that believes that she only deserves second best. The father who constantly nags his son to become more involved in sports though the son has absolutely no interest may be a person whose shadow side wishes that he was a success on the sporting field. The mother who criticises her daughter for not being pretty, slim or well-dressed enough may be a person who is battling with a shadow side that secretly resents the attention that her daughter receives and pines for the attention the father failed to give her.

The man with a shadow that is jealous and obsessive can come to light when he accuses his partner of being unfaithful to him, not loving him enough or not paying him enough attention. Maybe he is the one who is prone to being unfaithful, unloving and inattentive. He would not accept this of course but these traits may be hidden in his shadow side. You can sometimes feel very in adequate by the success and achievements of others. Unfortunately because success is generally measured in terms of educational prowess, financial rewards, status or visible documentation, other people who are just as successful in other ways can feel that their worth is not appreciated or valued as much. This can lead to people feeling that they are being overshadowed by others.

Edel hated school and so left at an early age. She is very artistic, creative and imaginative. She comes from an academic background and her brothers and sisters went the path of their parents and got degrees. The fact that Edel did not is a bone of contention with her parents who constantly sing the praises of their other children and almost apologise for Edel. As a result her self esteem is very low and she feels that she is second best. She also feels overshadowed by her brother and sisters. Simon is very athletic, loves sport and has excelled on the rugby pitch. Jack, on the other hand, lacks co-ordination and feels that he lives in the shadow of Simon. No amount of reassurance from his parents and his friends can convince him that he has much to offer in other ways. He often gets the impression that Simon knows this and plays the success game both on and off the pitch.

If you want your shadow side to dance along beside you on a sunny day maybe you need to address what is it really like when the sun go down. Ask yourself what part of yourself is it that brings you down, threatens you, hurts you and leads to confusion and pain. Perhaps start off with confiding in one that you trust, revealing your self honestly and directly. This is the life blood of intimacy. It may feel strange at the start, and almost artificial, but stick with it and decide and develop your own style. Learn to appreciate the full you, the lighter and the darker sides. Learn the value of putting things into words and get an understanding of what is happening to you in different situations.

Over-involvement with others can be the excess of the immature. It can be an involvement that is made by those who do not really understand themselves. They can become totally wrapped up with others, without ever really looking at themselves. Immature people usually get involved in immature relationships which often result in tantrums, sulks and the like. Very often, a person's motivation in a relationship is entirely different to those of their partner. Failure can occur when the needs of either partner are not being met. One person may want excitement or the buzz of a new sexual encounter, the other may crave love and security. This is a definite mismatch. Then again, a lot of people confuse love with being in love, never considering the reality of a real relationship. A relationship can end very quickly when the reality of a situation becomes clear.

Take, for example Matthew. He has been married for the past 30 years and he and his wife have a reasonably good marriage. But he is now at the stage where he is craving the excitement, fun and adventure of his youth and he has begun to see his wife Maeve as boring, staid and safe. Though part of him thrives on this security, his shadow side is screaming for recognition and he is spending more time out with his colleagues from work, living it up in restaurants and night-clubs.

Other relationships can leave us feeling let down short-changed, resentful and inadequate. In reality and it can be a cold reality for some, perfect relationships are as much an illusion as perfect love. Relationships involve trying to confront and manage as best we can our own vulnerabilities and anxieties.

We need to get acquainted with the self at every level before we start sorting someone else out. Relationships demand energy, time, commitment and compromise involving both good and difficult times.

A good relationship demands good ingredients. Qualities like honesty, loyalty, dependability and trust all ensure a smooth journey. To improve our own relationships with others perhaps we need to look at our own shadows before we leap into the shadows of others that lead us to nowhere.

6. Secrets

Have you got skeletons in your closet?

Can you remember the first time that anybody asked you to keep a secret. "I'll tell you something if you promise not to tell anybody". It may have been as a little child and you may have giggled and chuckled in the schoolyard with your pals about your common secrets. You may have felt special, trusted or chosen. You may have felt that you had a special bond with the person who asked you to keep the secret, as if you were in possession of something that was special or exciting.

So many secrets can be fun and innocent and they may even bring you happiness and joy. You may have a secret place where you can feel safe and free. You can have a secret diary where you pour out all your dreams, hopes and ambitions. You can have secret fantasies. Equally you may have addictions that you wish to keep secret. You may be a secret drinker, spender, eater or gambler. You may have a secret lover. Secretly you may be gay. You may have done something in your past that you want to remain a secret. You may have had an abortion. You may have given a child up for adoption, been fired from a job, been in trouble with the guards, failed important exams. In fact it could be anything. Also what may be a secret for some may not be for another. People have different value systems. There are so many secrets that are perfectly innocent and do not pose a problem for some but to others can become a burden.

Consider Gerry, Jackie and Elaine who have been life-long friends. They have shared many experiences, happy, enjoyable and some sad. Gerry and Elaine fell in love and got married and it was a terrible shock to Jackie. When she later found out that Elaine was being unfaithful to Gerry, Elaine begged her to keep it a secret. She has often pretended to Gerry that she and Elaine had been out together when in fact she was out with her lover.

Jackie feels very guilty when Gerry asks her if they had a good time, and the secret has become a terrible burden for her. She is afraid that she will let something slip and that Gerry will find out and as well as being furious with his wife he will also be furious with Jackie. She resents Elaine for making her privy to this information. She feels caught in a web of deceit.

Sandra had an abortion some years ago. This is a dark secret for her. She feels terribly saddened by this and also terribly ashamed and believes that people would see her differently if they ever found out. She has only told a very small group of people about this and if the subject of abortion ever comes up in conversation she feels very uncomfortable as if her secret is being wrenched from her.

Kenneth was always a very studious child and worked hard to ensure a place for himself at university. When he finished his degree with first class honours he succeeded in getting a job with a large multinational company. Initially he enjoyed his work and did not mind putting in long hours and spending time in the office. However, as time went on he began to feel as if he could do better somewhere else, and his enthusiasm waned. This change in his work was noticed by his employers who initially reprimanded, disciplined and eventually sacked him for other misdeanours. Kenneth was devastated. He realised that jobs, especially the ones he wanted were quite difficult to come by and he deeply regretted how things turned out at work. His family and friends were all quite established in their chosen careers, and though Kenneth was usually quick to turn to these people when he had any problems, he felt totally unable to tell them what happened. He felt ashamed, embarrassed, guilty, belittled and worthless — the whole gamut of negative emotions left him unable to confide in those close to him. Kenneth embarked on a whole game of pretence. He pretended that everything was normal, getting up as if going to work, meeting friends on a Friday for after-work drinks. He continued on doing the things he always did. On the occasions that he was asked about what was going on at work, he had a stock of answers at the ready. Outwardly, nobody noticed any difference in Kenneth; inwardly he was living in fear that his secret would be found out, fear of scorn and that he could not continue the charade, emotionally or financially.

Brenda became pregnant when she was 19. At the time she felt that the only option open to her was to give her child up for adoption. The father didn't want to have anything to do with the child. She was terrified of her parents discovering her dilemna. The social climate was closed to the idea of a single mother bringing up children on her own and added to all this she had little financial security. She later married and went on to have two children. Her family has no idea of what happened and she lives in fear that the child she gave up for adoption so long ago may try to find her. This is the secret that Brenda lives with.

Adolescence can be shrouded in secrecy. Girls and boys are just becoming aware of their sexuality. Secrets can be passed on about secret admirers, secret fantasises and secret meetings. Things that are done privately, for example exploring your body can be a close secret. There can sometimes be an element of shame surrounding things that are done in secret. People can also feel very let down if things that they held dearly and told others in total confidence are held up for scrutiny. For instance people who tell friends secrets and who later part with those friends can often be afraid that the person will go on to break their confidences. Also there can be a huge struggle with conscience when a person considers breaking a secret. Those who are able to keep secrets are seen as loyal and true, while those who break them are seen as weak, fickle and two-faced. But when is it ever right to break a secret?

Let's look at the dilemma that Eileen faced recently. Her son confessed to her that he had been in a house burglary which resulted in the owner suffering a heart attack shortly afterwards and dying. Her son begged her to keep this a secret and not to turn him in to the gardaí. He promised faithfully never to be involved in crime again. Eileen is torn between her desire to see justice done and her abhorrence of crime and her love for her son. After much soul-searching, she decided to keep the secret.

She believes that this will be a skeleton in the closet forever. We are all familiar with family secrets. They can bond a family together or they can break them apart. They can be used to insult and belittle a person and are often hurled at a person in a heated argument. Dermot is a recovering gambler. His addiction led him on a road of crime and debt. He and his family are well respected in their neighbourhood and they kept his problems a closely guarded secret. Though they have helped him in his fight to beat the addiction, rows often boil over and his secret is thrown in his face.

These secrets can even go to the grave and the person may have suffered much trauma during their lifetime, always fearing that somebody will find out or fearful of letting their guard down and letting something slip.

In cases of sexual abuse and incest, particularly with young children, the abuser usually tells the child that what is taking place is their little secret. Even though the child may instinctively know that what is going on is wrong he or she may trust the abuser. He/she may even be afraid of the abuser who has warned him never to talk. People who are harbouring burdensome secrets can become very secretive in other areas of their lives and be perceived as cute or sly. People who live with secrets and have become accustomed to hiding things can sometimes live in denial. The secret drinker can pretend that he/she doesn't have a problem, not only to herself but also to others and go on to continue to damage themselves in secret. Secret love affairs typify all that goes with secret living, the secret meetings, the secret phonecalls, the secret nights together, the secret memories. Life can become a merry-go-round of lies and deceit. There is the constant fear of being found out, being seen together, receipts being found, phone calls being disturbed, pregnancy or maybe even blackmail.

Joe who is married became attracted to Jane who worked with him. Though they both were aware of the chemistry between them, they initially had no real intention of becoming involved. But late night meetings, drinks with colleagues after work and conferences abroad ensured that they were thrown together and the attraction grew. Joe became totally besotted with Jane and began to meet her secretly. Though he has grown to care about her very deeply he is not prepared to leave his wife. He does not want to hurt her but he has no qualms about telling Jane that his marriage is a sham. He tells his wife that he is working late to cover up his late nights. He is now at the stage that he has told so many lies to both that he almost now enjoys all the attention shown to him by both of them. His girlfriend pities him as she genuinely believes that his wife is giving him a hard time and his wife feels sorry for him as she believes that he is overstretched at work. They both have ended up putting more into their relationship with him than he has with them.

Maurice and Jessica have been having an affair for the last three years. Both are in love and terrified that their secret will be discovered. They first met when Maurice, who is a priest began to do some voluntary work at the school where Jessica teaches. Both of them feel very stressed and under pressure with the veil of secrecy that surrounds their liaison. They are constantly on their guard and on the rare occasions when they go on holidays together they fear that they will bump into somebody that they know. As they love each other, it is natural that they want to talk about each other and Jessica finds this particularly difficult. There have been many times in the school staffroom that she has had to bite her tongue when her colleagues talk about their husbands and boyfriends. Maurice has to battle with his feelings of guilt arising from his life as a priest and lover.

Illness may also be something that a person feels that he or she must keep secret. For example a person may hide the fact that he or she has been in a psychiatric hospital. A person with aids may be terrified of the stigma, fear and misunderstanding that surrounds the illness and so keeps it a secret. It was even common years ago for people to keep quiet about having a child with a physical handicap and the secret itself was after mental anguish.

Barbara and Edward always appeared as the "perfect couple". To any onlooker they appeared to have it all — wealth, looks, two adorable children and a wonderful social life.

However little did anyone know of Barbara's dark secret. Unknown to their wide social circle Edward enjoyed dressing up in women's clothes. Barbara simply loathed his "dressing up" together with the money he spent on make up and female clothing. Barbara went along with it for "peace" but she hated having to lie to her friends and pretend she and Edward had a great personal relationship. Edward adopted a "take me for what I am" attitude and avoided confrontation. Their secret, in fact, places a huge burden not only on themselves but also their children who always sense a tense atmosphere.

Going to counselling or therapy for the first time can be extremely traumatic for some. When you are asked to reveal part of yourself you may feel that you are being stripped down and you feel extremely vulnerable. Revealing the contents of your past, your dreams, and fears may make you feel that you are letting a secret part of you out. You can feel helpless, inadequate, powerless and even disloyal to your secrets. This in turn can create tensions between you and your therapist until you know that it's safe to talk and that your secrets will be both respected, protected and that your inner world will not be destroyed. Because you feel that you would have nothing left inside if you let it all out, you may sometimes hold on until such time that you believe that letting go will open up a whole new dimension for you. Because secrecy has been, in a strange way, a comforting way of breaking off a traumatic experience as well as blanking out reality it is vital that you face it.

Perhaps the following tools might help to unload the burden of secrets. Give yourself a break and examine the secrets that you're holding. Look at the hurt that they may be causing you and others. They may be the source of much of your stress, hurt and fear and that letting them go may relieve you of all this burden. There are many therapists that you can talk to in total confidence about your secrets. The therapists may be able to get you to look at your secrets in a different light and this may help to free you and lighten your load. There is a wonderful sense of freedom about being able to talk openly and unburden yourself from painful emotions.

You may also have to make a decision. If you are involved in a secretive relationship, perhaps its time to make a decision about your relationship. You may want to continue or indeed end the relationship, but the decision is yours. If the secrecy of the relationship is causing you heartache or weighing too heavily on your mind then it may be time to let go of this terrible weight. Look at also the people who are affected by your secret liaison and who may be hurt.

Secrets eventually catch up on you and you can become shrouded in the burden of pain and also the responsibility of keeping your secret safe from others. It leaves you with a sense of inner turmoil that peeps through when you feel that your secret might be let out of the bag. Don't go around with a heaviness inside you saying. "you never know the day when your secret will be disclosed". Avoid burying your head in the sand and hoping your secret will dissolve like the pebbles on the beach. Some people even live life knowing that their secret will only be safe when they go to their grave. Let go and let happiness shine through. It is time you gave your inner self a break from secrecy.

7. The pain of isolation

Living on the Outside

"I'm lonely" is not something that people, for many different reasons, can admit too easily. They can be afraid that people will pity them, will try to include them in events out of guilt and not the desire to be in their company or perhaps view them as bad mixers and unsociable. It is important to state that there is a very big difference between "being lonely" and "being alone". Some people relish the idea of spending time alone, away from work, stress, targets, pressure, deadlines or maybe even home. They can enjoy this immensely and do things that they want to do instead of fitting in with what others want. But for others, the very thought of being alone could fill them with anxiety and one which in itself could lead to a very stressful situation. It is also true that one could be surrounded by people and still experience the pain of loneliness. The reasons for loneliness are as varied as the underlying issues that are at work in the person's own personality.

Perhaps your first experience of feeling lost was as a child when you were separated from your parents on a shopping trip. I am sure that you can still remember the awful feelings of panic, fear and abandonment. Feeling lost can be something that a person can experience for a number of reasons. It could be that you feel lost after the death of a partner or parent. You could feel lost if you have been made redundant from a job, if you have separated from your partner, if you have retired, if your children have left home, if you have moved to another part of the country or indeed moved to a new country or if you have started a new job.

Death is so final and often so unprepared for and unexpected that it can leave the remaining partner or friend feeling so traumatised that they are unable to articulate their sadness and their fears for the future. They may be frightened that they will never again have the wonderful bond of closeness and security. They may be afraid of facing the future with out this person in their lives. Immediately following the death of a person, other people rally round and help, but as time goes on the bereaved person is left alone with their grief and may sometimes feel that people's capacity to listen and be sympathetic may have a limit and this only serves to further increase their isolation. There is very often a mixed message during the time of bereavement. Hundreds arrive for the funeral and two months down the road, when reality sets in, the person left behind can feel very isolated and on their own with no shoulder to cry on.

Loss, isolation and loneliness are all interwoven. People can fear that they will never be able to recover from the situation and feel that their lives are never going to be the same. Some are so badly affected that they feel suicidal. They feel as if there is no escape. Health suffers for others. Joan lost her husband after thirty nine years of happy marriage. Even though he had been ill for some time, Joan was totally unprepared for the awful ache that she felt after he died. She felt as if part of her had been cut off and that nobody could really understand what she was going through. She often wishes that death would come to her too so that she would be reunited with her husband.

It can often be immensely sad for those who have experienced a loss of any kind to see others who are with people that they love. They can feel left out and unwanted and also somehow envious of the happiness of others. We live in a culture that is very much geared towards couples and people can be left out of situations because of this. Eileen is very shy and feels uncomfortable with large groups of people. On the occasions that she does go to parties she feels almost paralysed by her fear of talking to strangers and now opts out of going to social engagements. She feels very lonely and cut off but her fear of speaking to strangers is greater than her fear of being alone.

Clodagh was engaged to Brian for five years. He ended their engagement and began to see another woman. Clodagh was devastated and began to build up information on his new girlfriend. She has convinced her friends to go to the pubs, restaurants and other outlets that his new love goes to. They sit and watch as Brian laughs and has fun with his new girlfriend. Interestingly, even though this is painful for Clodagh she gets a feeling of closeness to her ex by being in the places that the new girlfriend goes and she would feel very lost if she stopped going. There are many situations when you feel that you can talk about these feelings of loneliness and isolation, but there are people who cannot bring themselves to mention anything. They may be in denial that anything is really wrong and they may become negative in their attitude and lose complete interest in their appearance and their future. This in turn becomes a vicious circle as the more isolated and negative they feel, the more that they are left to their own devices and feel even more outside. The stress and fear of isolation can sap your energy and leave you bereft of the strength and vitality that you may need to pull yourself out of the darkness.

There is also the loneliness associated with being different in society. Unemployment, handicap, homosexuality and poverty each has its own accompanying stress. People who have feelings of shame or guilt can feel isolated by their need to hide and they are very aware of the stigma attached. Take for example a woman who has left a religious order. She may be afraid of the stigma that goes along with opting out and she feel outside what is socially acceptable. Society puts an onus on people to be the same and those who are not can get left behind, and they may not be backed up by society. Someone who has chosen to marry a person from a different culture can often feel as if they are living on the fringes and that they don't fit in. They can feel marginalised and this leads to them being isolated. People can very often turn to drink, drugs, food or excessive spending to help them block out the loneliness and anaesthetise their feelings.

Amanda has been separated for the last two years. Though she is happy to acknowledge that her marriage was not working, she has been very sad that her dreams of a happy and fulfilling marriage have not been realised. She has started to drink heavily to help her get through the lonely nights. But her drinking has alienated her from her friends who feel that she is a different person under the influence of alcohol and they don't always want to be around her. This in turn has increased her sense of being alone and dampened her self-worth. She has become a recluse and her only friend is the bottle.

Peggy is 83. She has lived a very full and active life and travelled extensively, enjoying many wonderful experiences. In later life she returned to university and studied for a PhD in philosophy. As far as her neighbours were concerned she was distant and removed. This was not the impression that Peggy wanted to convey but it was the idea that the neighbours, rightly or wrongly, chose to adopt. As Peggy got older this impression was compounded. She could not get out and about as much and was less visible in the community. Peggy has been quite hurt and saddened by her neighbours harshness and in a sense she has now almost become defensive and hostile towards them and this has a knock on effect. Peggy spends much of her time alone . Most of her peers have died and she passes the time watching neighbourly camaraderie from her window. So now as well as being seen as lofty, people now choose to think Peggy is nosy.

Unemployment can have a terrible effect on an individual's psychological and physical well being. The unemployed can go through the experience of feeling that they are not at one with the rest of society and they can be further marginalised by the fact that they don't have the money to go out and socialise. Its a catch-22 for many as even the cost of getting CVs printed up, the cost of telephone calls and the price of stamps can be a headache for them. Thus they may have to forego the opportunity of even getting an application form to prospective employers. They also have to try to fill in long empty days and battle with bills and finances.

Brendan has been unemployed since being made redundant from his job as a factory worker. He has become used to watching his neighbours getting ready to leave for work in the mornings and he feels as if everybody has passed him by. His days are spent lying in bed until the afternoon and watching television. He has no money for much socialising and he dreads the night time as it is then that the worries he has about trying to bring up his two children come to the surface. He gets very lonely and feels lost and frightened when he goes to do his shopping and is surrounded with people who seem to be happy and secure. He wonders will he ever be part of the work force again.

The loss of a once-valued friend, through death or emigration for instance can leave a big gap in a person's life and cause them much loneliness. They can literally feel cut-up and raw just like the person who loses a beloved spouse. They may feel that they never again will have such a close, warm bond. They are envious sometimes when they watch other people enjoying a night out in the company of their friends and see these people as being wanted and supported.

Nicholas is gay. When his partner died, his family and friends rallied round and offered solace, support and sympathy. However, when time elapsed and when the real ache of loneliness set in, Nicholas' support network seemed to disappear and he was alone with his grief. He felt as if all the offers of help and company were easier for people to forget and that they wanted to be able to enjoy their own happiness, without the reminder of his unhappiness.

As we get older and retire from our jobs, there can be a very strong sense of loss, particularly a loss of belonging. For many years, a person toils at their work and grows accustomed to the daily routine that goes along with it. Their day is mapped out and the time that is put aside for leisure is valued and precious but when the tables are turned and the leisure time is freely available they may feel lost and alone. Those people in employment have a network of colleagues and work associates and feel part of the wider team. The shock of facing days without the constant and urgent demand on one's time can have a very serious effect on how a person sees themselves. They may miss the camaraderie of mingling with work colleagues, the work itself and the role they had in the company. Even the drop in living standards may prove difficult to come to terms with. The person many find it very difficult to become used to quietness and relaxation — of having a lot of time on his or her hands. It is therefore very important that a person plans for their retirement, and becomes involved in other activities that are rewarding and give satisfaction and pleasure and a sense of involvement. People who are still working may also feel isolated from those they work with. A person in a high-powered position who feels that the responsibility is weighing too heavily may believe that he or she is cut off from those in different grades.

Sometimes too the person may even long for a lesser position so that it may be possible to blend in, be one of the gang and enjoy the office gossip. The person may believe that he or she is being judged all the time and cannot afford to put a foot wrong. This, in itself, can be very isolating. Pressure mounts, the person feels stressed and stress can in itself provoke feelings of isolation. If a person feels that they cannot cope, they may have to take time out to deal with this and may feel as if they have to do all this on their own. They may crave the support and inclusiveness that their work provides. It may have been a long time since the person really looked at themselves. They may not always like what they see and thus more isolation and loneliness may follow. There are also people who shy away from taking too many holidays, or time alone, dreading the idea of being alone with their thoughts. Lonely people are often like little branches in a tree. They can feel very fragile and open to the cold winds which blow them around.

When a situation arises, a person may be completely unprepared for the unexpected and wish that they had a warning of what was to come. Any new situation — even advancement — can bring on feelings of isolation, threat and fear. Fear is a big issue for all of us. It can be the thing that binds us to our past and locks us into a world from which we are afraid to break free. We seem to have the idea that tomorrow will bring us happiness and contentment and that today is just the rehearsal. We have to realise that tomorrow may never dawn for us. Today is precious by the very fact that we are here to enjoy it.

We must realise that we have often to make our own happiness and nobody can actually give us the fountain of happiness that is so vital. Laughter is a great form of therapy. When did you laugh, really laugh. Research shows that adults do not laugh with the same abandon that children do. They do not dance with life in the same way that little ones do. They do not seem to have the same wonder and zest for life. They are bogged down with the stress of life and sometimes take it all too seriously. To help avoid creating more stress it is important that we learn to recognise what is going on in our lives. We must take heed of the warnings — the flashing lights. It is vital that you can talk about how you feel. This can ease away the awful ache of loneliness and may help you to discover new paths of discovery and hope.

If, for some reason, you should be embarrassed to confide in someone you know, and you are aware that you need professional help, then seek it. Sharing our fears, anxieties and worries can be a lightening of a terrible load and there are many areas of help open to us today so don't bottle things up. Be kind and patient with yourself and allow yourself the time and understanding to move forward. Try to prioritise what is really important and ask yourself what do you need. Get support. Learn to pace yourself. There is nothing wrong in doing things at a slow pace, like the snail you will eventually get there and things do take time. Remember that there is no right or wrong way to do things and each to his or her own. Everyone is different and what works for one person may not be so effective for another, so it is imperative to do what is good and right for you. Realise that if you feel a sense of loss, it is necessary to acknowledge this. It is alright to say that you will never get over your loss, whatever it may be but do remember that it is possible to deal with it and learn to cope. Above all, realise that things will get brighter and lighter. There is always some further happiness out there so try and find yours.

If you have no job seek all the help available and be prepared to look at alternatives routes. Structure your day as best you can to avoid boredom or monotony. Remember, this life is not a dress rehearsal. Everyday must be enjoyed. If at first you don't succeed always remember there are other options open to you.

PART II:

KNOW YOURSELF: THE COPING SELF

8. Meeting your needs

Finding fulfilment

I know what you need. I know what's good for you. Does this sound familiar. It seems that all through our lives there is no shortage of people telling us what we need or more to the point what they think we need. This has the result of confusing us. As children, our needs are simple. We needed to be fed, changed, to sleep, to be loved, cared for and to be held. As we got older, though, our basic needs remain the same. We change in the way that we need fulfilment, financial security, challenges, new experiences, stability in fact, lots of various things. Some people are very good at getting their needs met. They are very good at knowing what they want and they are equally good at vocalising their needs. On the other hand, there are those who never tune in to what they need. They can even believe that they don't have the right to get their needs met. They may then spend all their time meeting the needs of others. When you look at all the people who have sacrificed their chance of happiness to lead lives contrary to their expectations, you may get a picture of what this chapter is all about.

Of course it is admirable to care and look out for others, but if a person is doing this to the detriment of oneself, then something is wrong. It could even be that they feel that they will only be loved and special if they constantly meet the needs of others and there are the people who fall into the trap of being a martyr to other people's needs. It can be a way of avoiding their own. Or sometimes it can be a control factor. If they are always looking after others there can be an element of control, even at an unconscious level.

For instance, Alexia has spent practically her entire life living with her parents. As they got older she threw all her energy and commitment in to ensuring that they could never want for anything. Relatives and friends marvelled at her dedication and love for her parents and she was constantly praised by both her Mum and Dad. In fact, this may be a very clever ploy by Alexia. She craves attention and believes that she will never get on in life, either professionally, emotionally or financially. She feels that by staying at home with her parents, she can be excused for not having reached a certain stage of material and financial security. She is having some of her needs met by the attention that is shown to her through the care of her parents. Other people pay her attention and she has the constant devotion of her Mum and Dad all the time.

Martha is 10. She loves the rough and tumble of playing with the boys and has no time at all for what she considers to be the feminine things, like dolls, frilly dresses and playing house, preferring instead all sorts of innocent devilment with the boys and is considered a tomboy. Her mother has always wanted a little girl, and had three boys before Martha came along. She adores getting dressed up and always looks very glamorous. She always thought that if she had a little girl it would be wonderful to get her all dressed up looking like a little doll. She needs to be admired and, as such, she needs her little Martha to be admired too. She feels that the child is not meeting her expectations and those of others. So Martha's mum is trying to live out her hopes and needs through her child. She sees her child as a means of getting some of her needs met and battles with Martha who wants to be one of the boys at all times.

At twelve Paul is a shy and reticent child. He is very sensitive and hates confrontation. His hobbies are reading, fishing and art. These hobbies are solitary activities and he is perfectly happy being on his own. His father though loves being the centre of attention and is always in the thick of things. He constantly pesters Paul to accompany him to rugby matches which the child detests and this causes confrontation, much to his dismay. His own father needed to do the things that he considered to be the normal familial activities and he too is trying to achieve this through his son. In many ways he is trying to relive his youth through Paul.

Children have a need to satisfy their natural sense of fun, curiosity and adventure. This can instil great confidence and help to develop coping skills. If parents stifle this natural need and smother their children, the child may never go on to make his or her own mistakes and may end up shy, insecure and lacking in confidence. If on the other hand, the parents encourage the child to make his/her own way in the world with a sense of wonder and excitement, the child will grow up with confidence, self-assurance and the ability to cope with awkward situations.

Jimmy is eight and an only child. His parents are very protective of him and believe that nobody can look after and care for him as well as they do. He has grown accustomed to his parents protecting him from life and believes that the world is very dangerous and unsafe — which is what his parents have drummed in to him. One of his parents always collects him from school, not trusting anybody else with this task. One day through a mixture of bad communication and misunderstanding, no one turned up at the school gates to bring him home. Jimmy became hysterical and was inconsolable. He firmly believed that his parents had come to some harm, and that he in turn would too. Eventually, it was all sorted out, but it could have turned out differently. Of course Jimmy's parents need to educate him to the dangers that are undoubtedly in the world but he doesn't need to be constantly terrified by his parents warnings and heedings of bad events. His parents have a duty to look out for his needs and to help make his world safer, but by smothering him they are ensuring that he will grow up to be suspicious and to feel threatened and unsafe.

It is important for parents and even potential parents to realise that they cannot live out their needs and their lives through their children. Everyone has to make his or her way in this world. Everyone has choices, and though life may sometimes be an uncertain adventure, it is our adventure and nobody has the right to limit or stifle us. While we all need support and care, it should not be at someone else's expense.

Some needs can be used as an excuse not to examine things

that cause us pain in our lives. Paula has a need to always appear organised and under control. She feels that if she lets this veneer down people will see her as just another ordinary person and she needs to feel that she is in someway better than others. There is a great reluctance in people to accept the need for change. "I want to change, but I don't know how or I don't know where to start" is a defeatist attitude and signals a reluctance to take a risk. Many people put up with things that they know they should change but fear often keeps them there. It keeps them shackled to things that are not doing them any good and prevents them from moving on.

We should try to look at what we enjoy, what makes us happy. We need to learn that it is alright to show vulnerability and we all have a need and a hunger for change because we need to unravel and examine the mixed messages that our needs can send us. We also have to accept that we have different needs at different stages in our lives. Let us take a look at just some of the things that we say as a matter of habit.

- I need to get the house ready before a friend arrives.

- I need to get ready and look presentable before so-and-so comes.

- I need to make the bed before I go out in the morning.

- I need to go on a diet/lose weight.

- I need to stop spending so much money.

We spend so much time wrapped up in these things that the question must be asked as to whose needs are actually being met? Is the world going to fall apart because the bed is not made, if the sitting room looks a mess, if you don't always look a million dollars. We have to realise that life is too short to be worried about things that are not urgent. Think of all the time that you spend projecting about what you should be doing. Instead turn all this energy around and make the things that really matter happen for you. Also you will realise that the world will not come asunder if you take some time out. Stop trying to do everything. No one is superhuman and, equally, no one is indispensable. Practice prioritising and using your energy wisely.

Laura needs a holiday to unwind and to relax, but she feels insecure about her job. She is afraid that if she goes somebody will be brought in her place and will prove to be better than she is and perhaps take her job. Some people's needs are so strong that they get mixed up with their own insecurities and result in them using their weakness as a form of weapon. It could be the elderly parent who resents her daughter or son leaving home and claims that he or she cannot possibly manage without her. This is a very selfish way of getting needs met and can mean that the son or daughter who does actually leave is ridden with guilt. In personal relationships too, people can weave and manipulate others to get their needs met. This is basically akin to being dishonest as the person is actually afraid to voice their needs, and instead looks to achieve them in an underhand way. There can be serious consequences. It can result in their friends, parents, partners or children resenting them for manipulating them and it can also leave the person resenting the fact that they cannot be open about their needs.

We all have the same needs, but people differ in the ability to fulfil them. When you fail to satisfy a need, you can often compensate by having an abundance of something else. For instance a person may desperately need love and affection, and instead can have a wonderful standard of living with all the material trappings. This can be used to satisfy the craving for another's love. Parents who fail to spend enough time with their children often indulge and spoil them. This can exonerate the parents from giving the time to the children and they may feel that instant gratification will suffice. This, however, postpones the closeness and attention that the children need. One of our most basic needs is the need to be valued. Without this, a person can end up feeling isolated, inadequate and unloved. People are not objects. They are not puppets on a string, and from an early age we must learn to respect and value our lives and those of others.

We all need to feel a bond with our fellow man/woman in some way and to have a sense of being at home both emotionally and physically. This provides a foundation for other needs. However, it is the need for intimacy that must be addressed in a wider framework. Couples today may have to provide the emotional intimacy that society and the community at large has left behind.

Sometimes, though, in this commercial and media-driven world, we can confuse intimacy with sex and there are often some very strong mixed messages. Intimacy involves emotional, mental and physical closeness with another person together with openness and honesty. However very often the two get intertwined and tangled and we can confuse sex with satisfying an emotional need and end up feeling betrayed, let down, used or abused. We are led to believe that we need everything now. Everything is instant and this can even include sex. "If you don't have sex with me, I'm leaving" is often the emotional blackmail that is used by people in couples to get what they want. People want happiness now and they want it most in their intimate relationships.

The intimacy and closeness of our most cherished relationships often represents our whole belief in ourselves and we are conscious of, and vulnerable to the image we portray to our loved ones. Sometimes we choose a partner believing and hoping that they can give us all the love, care and support that we need. Initially, this may happen and it can be a wonderful and joyous feeling but when the bubble bursts and the honeymoon is over, we realise that we may not be getting what we hoped for. We can start to look for the flaws and cracks in the relationship. This can bring a great deal of unhappiness as each partner struggles to regain the initial euphoria and realises the need to make one's own happiness, rather than expecting another person to fulfil this need. Partners can end up being guarded with each other. They may stop sharing and confiding and may withdraw and stop listening. They may live in silence. They then feel isolated, without the support of the other and this can lead to an emotional void caused by the lack of empathy, understanding and compassion that both partners need in order to sort out the turmoil and mixed messages.

Eventually they may not even know where to begin. All the classic statements come into play: "I don't know what you need"; "I don't understand you"; "How do you expect me to help when you don't know what you want"; "You're all the same, selfish and spoilt"; "You think only of yourself". The first step very often is to seek help together to try and rebuild and re-establish the relationship. You may have to start all over again and express your thoughts, wishes and desires and begin to listen to each other. If you can do this without the help of a third party, then start now rather than waiting until it is too late. You both need to open up and begin to share together. You need to let go of too high expectations and grudges. Understand your needs, hopes, wishes, beliefs, weaknesses and strengths. It is vital to know the beliefs that you have because if you don't you may transfer them to your partner. Don't punish yourself any more. Learn, explore and enjoy what the other person wants and find new ways to meet both of your needs. Bonding is a valid need that doesn't weaken a person but makes them stronger. Taking pleasure in each other is a habit that some couples have to acquire and taking and giving pleasure to each other is very often the thing that you both want.

Maura's children have all left home and started out on their own. She invested most of her life bringing them up, and neglected friends, hobbies and outside interests. She now feels totally alone and unneeded and in a way she resents her children for leaving her, though she is delighted that they are able to stand on their own two feet. She now has the opportunity to re-establish her relationship with her husband which she neglected when the children were younger.

In life we all have to answer to our true self. When someone or something is upsetting us get to the root and sort out the problem as soon as possible. Don't allow your needs to be caught up in a web of mixed messages that leaves you endlessly distinguishing fact from fantasy.

Fantasy can be a way of coping when certain needs are not

met. We day-dream, wish and desire for something that may never become a reality. Sometimes this is done through the haze of alcohol, only to wake up the next morning feeling the emptiness and the realisation that fact conquers fantasy and what you thought might be is not possible.

The realisation maybe the jolting factor to put you back on the rails and get your real needs met. It may be painful initially but with time you may get the opportunity to strive towards your goal akin to bringing your fantasy into the world. Never give up. Make the effort until it becomes effortless.

Work on your own needs, but try also to understand that others may vary in their expectations, demands, requests and realisations.

9. Signs, Symbols or Status?

Inward or outward Show

Each era brings with it its own stamp of what the perfect lifestyle is. There are so many things to denote outward show. It may be the food we eat, the clothes that we wear, the area that we live in or the pubs and restaurants that we frequent. People have always adapted music, food, clothes to suit the times. Last year's fashionable wine may now be seen as passi and for those who are ruled by fashion there is nothing more unsettling that to find that they are out of touch. Fashion, be it in music or clothes can also signal a revolution. Back in the sixties the songs of Bob Dylan and Joan Baez were often playing in the background when young people got together to bemoan the state of governments the world over. The clothes that were worn in those days signalled the vibrancy, the lack of restriction and the freedom that the era represented.

Society's economic and cultural trends sway us in the choices of what we buy. We are often fickle and we need to feel that we are "in". We only have to look at the whole fashion and cosmetic industries to see how we can be seduced into buying an illusion, a dream of attainable perfection, but only if we buy such and such a brand or wear a particular label. Some people are more concerned with the labels on a coat rather than its efficiency in keeping out the inclement weather. People who do not go along with the flow can be classified as "fuddy duddies", or simply out of date. Suddenly we want to shake off our previously ideals and values. It's off with the old and on with the new. Remember we all end up in the same place when we are finally laid to rest.

Oscar Wilde may have had a point when he said that youth is wasted on the young. We can all look back and remember being in a hurry to grow up. Young people perceive being grown up as taking control and doing what one wants to do. As we get older, we soon realise that there are many decisions to be made and demands to be met. When we enter the workforce, we meet up with juniors, apprentices, trainees, assistants and novices. The young are usually impatient and anxious to move up the corporate ladder. They long for the privileges attached to rank and power but don't realise the prerogatives of being in a junior position, of being at the bottom. Junior status gives us the opportunities for support, the right to sometimes make mistakes and to take advice. No one is threatened by us and this serves to protect us. Later when we acquire senior status new responsibilities come our way together with new decision-making powers. We may not have the support any longer and people may now even feel threatened. There can also be gender issues to address.

For example, Carol became head of her department when she was 31. Instead of being seen as clever and ambitious she was perceived as a threat to her male co-workers. They thought of her as a rival, instead of a colleague and friend. Very often like growing older, changing status is a gradual and slow process. Sometimes we get so caught up in the web of status that it is only when something goes badly wrong that we are forced to stop and look at what is going on around us. Sometimes the transition from one position to another does not run as smoothly as we hope and expect. Acquiring a new home, a top-of-the-range car, promotion, even having children can so often be different from our earlier expectations and this can leave us feeling that we cannot cope with the demands that are being heaped upon us. We have to adjust to a new set of rules and a new way of life. Sometimes it can become a struggle and we long for the old and more familiar lifestyle.

Joan's husband was promoted at work and they decided as couple to move to a new area. It meant leaving behind the friends that they had built up, and the support of their neighbours and family. Though their new house was bigger and in a "better" area, they felt isolated and lonely. This situation can often set off ambivalent feelings because we are creatures of habit and readjusting can bring its own pain. It is like giving up the old security blanket that we had as children. We are delighted to get back to our own nests where we feel comfortable and free from putting on an act after a social event that we had to adopt a certain manner for.

Labels and status symbols have merited so much importance now that there is tremendous pressure being put on people to acquire all the latest gadgets, equipment and up-to-date clothes, accessories and designer labels. Expensive and exotic holidays are all the rage as people push out the boundaries to gain more and more. If a parent can afford to send their children to the best schools they can feel as if this will afford the children the entry into society that is seen as so important. This can be a terrible strain and a drain on parents. One feels that he or she must go along with what everybody else is doing and they feel that they will be looked down on if they don't fit it with this lifestyle.

Sandra and her husband Jerome do not like foreign holidays. They are happiest when they are touring around the west of Ireland and stopping off along the way to fish and enjoy a simple evening out. Their children are used to their schoolfriends going off on family holidays to foreign climes and they are now beginning to put pressure on their parents to take them away. Apart from the fact that Sandra and Jerome genuinely don't like travelling, they feel as if they have other things to spend their money on and give their children other experiences. They now feel that they may have to take a foreign trip simply because everybody else is doing so and don't want their children feeling left out. People can even feel obliged to get into debt to buy all the things that they see others acquiring. Think of the waste of time and energy and money that is spent on trying to keep up with the Jones's.

Jackie and her husband Karl got heavily into debt and were forced to sell their home. They both felt that they would not be accepted into the circles that they wanted to move in without the trappings that proclaimed that they had "made it". Strangely enough, they didn't in fact like their newly found friends and saw them as being false and stuck up, but they were caught up in the lifestyle and found it impossible to get out.

Inevitably when they couldn't afford to keep up the pretence any longer, their fair-weather friends deserted them. Karl and Jackie had to then sit down and look at what their real values really were. Sometimes we need to reassess our expectations, direction and choices and look at what is really important for us.

Lauren is friendly with people who gossip about, backbite and criticise her behind her back and generally look down on her. You might wonder why she chooses to associate with people like that. The answer is that she wishes to be involved with these people purely because they belong to the "right set". They have money, power and position and Lauren feels that by virtue of association, she will be respected and looked up to.

Years ago, the doctors, the priests and the teachers were among the people who were looked up to and held in esteem. They were treated with reverence and respect and none too little bowing and scraping. People who may not have been lucky enough to gain an education felt as if they were somehow subordinates and indeed many were made to feel as if they were just that. Things have moved on and education is thankfully more freely available to all. People whose forefathers and mothers may have been servants to the doctors, priests and teachers are now highly thought of in their own professions. Because things are, in a way, more equal there is less status attached to certain professions and less opportunity for some people to wield power and position. People who once may have been respected and valued by virtue of their rank in life are now being treated in a much more equitable way and respected by virtue of being human beings.

Maybe we need to examine what our new-found status is doing for us. What is a progressive or retrograde step? What is positive or negative for us? Does our place in society make a difference to how we feel about ourselves or how others see us? Do we really care about climbing the ladder to material and social success or indeed should we really care if we are not achieving the financial rewards that are perceived as necessary? Should we really be upset if the invitations to all the best parties are not flooding through our letterboxes, or that were not sporting the best designer clothes, sunglasses or perfume? Are you tolerating or enjoying your successes? It a noose a round your neck? Is it a welcoming or distancing sign? Give yourself permission to adjust to your new found status. Realise that it may not be what you expected. If you need to get out, then do so. Remember that you always have choices and that there is always something waiting for you, something more affirming and often more enjoyable. Feel free to be yourself and don't feel pressurised if you are not living up to someone else's standards. Don't be afraid to be your own person.

10. Nourishing the Self

Looking after You

When summer is over and the evenings begin to close in, many of us feel the need to do extra-curricular activities and may embark on evening classes. Some of us may want to learn to communicate better while others will follow up on courses like car maintenance, cooking or upholstery. Picture yourself when you bought your first car. This can be your pride and joy and you spend precious time cleaning and polishing it and keeping it spic and span. Looking after the exterior is, of course, the easiest part and many people never try to explore the inner workings. They may then be surprised to find their gleaming, spotless car letting them down from time to time. All the time and energy spent on keeping the outside looking good is wasted if you don't stop to examine the inside. It is the same with the self. We may spend time looking after our physical appearance, with scant regard for our emotional needs. Let's imagine that you are on a personal development course and on completion of this you will be awarded a certificate. You will be able to banish negativity, throw away emotional pain and give yourself confidence and above all, give yourself new found enjoyment, fulfilment and fun. Shall we start by examining what it is that blocks you from achieving contentment.

Blockages such as guilt, worry, anxiety, resentment, anger, self pity and remorse deplete energy levels and weigh us down. We are not free to be our own persons and these blockages are related to our feelings. Our feelings nestle inside us as an integral part of our emotional system. They are always sending us messages, yet we find it difficult to understand them and even may tend to ignore them. But they are always working for us, protecting us from damage by warning us that something is wrong. Some feelings can bring great joy, while others can overwhelm us and cause much pain. Sometimes there can be inner conflict for us which is akin to a mixed message.

Joanne just passed her exam and wants to share her joy with everyone. Unfortunately when she meets her boyfriend, she has to shift gears to empathise with him as he has not done quite so well. Later that evening, Joanne feels guilty about her mixed emotions and this self-induced guilt overshadows her happiness. When she tells her mother about this, she rebukes her by saying not to brag about your success as others may have failed too and think of how they must be feeling. The pay-off in guilt-ridden situations is that you can avoid responsibility and if you feel guilty for long enough, you will eventually convince yourself that you are exonerated for being bold or bad in some way. Worry causes the same havoc in our lives. Sometimes worry is equated with caring which is very confusing for the recipient.

It is quite amazing when we think, for instance, of the money that we lavish on keeping our physical appearance in good order. We are easily seduced by the luxury of expensive cosmetics. The fancy packaging and the extravagant claims lure us into believing that we will be transformed into glowing beauties if only we buy the hydrating baths, the balsams, nourishing masks and all the other treatments that are on offer. These are going to restore us, rejuvenate us and render us beautiful, serene and desired. Think then of the little time that we spend on ensuring that our emotional needs are being looked after. We give little time to relaxing and to enjoying doing nothing, to read, to walk, to visit places of beauty and tranquillity, to inform ourselves on what is going on in the world to enrich our minds and our thoughts, to take time to banish the fears and the cares that hinder us from enjoying peace, the time to see and recognise our talents, the time to realise when we are overdoing things. The list is long. Why do we spend such a short time nourishing our selves? When we think of the feelings that surround "being selfish", it becomes a little easier to understand and see why we don't spend the time we should nourishing the core self.

Selfishness, in the true and pure form is to be applauded. It is, quite literally, loving the self and it is nearly impossible to love others without firstly understanding and loving oneself. It is treating oneself with respect and appreciation and taking pride in what we do well. It is realising that we deserve care and love and it is only when we fully recognise these needs and rights that we can then go on to get other areas of our lives in order. In an age of technology when we are hell bent on finding instant cures to go with instant communication it is just as important to look inside ourselves and realise that we have many cures from inside in the form of our ability to overcome trials and tribulations together with our great coping strengths.

For instance, Jacinta is forever telling her daughter that she is worried about her staying out late at night. She tells her that she would not bother worrying if she did not care about her and that she should be glad that there are people to care about her. Jacinta tells her daughter that she must have little regard for her mother to worry her so much and that it is bad for her blood pressure. By doing this, Jacinta is transferring her worry onto her daughter who feels that she would be to blame if anything happened to her mother. This is an unfair burden on a young girl and it is all because Jacinta has not looked at the underlying reasons for her worry and instead continues to project them on to other people.

Of course, many of the things that we worry about never come true but no matter how rational we try to be, these worries can creep into our minds at the most inopportune times and we can torture ourselves turning them over and over again in our heads. Worry is one of the most damaging habits that we have in our lives. Worry is a very bad habit. Think about it. If you worry about something, will it actually change the outcome? You have spent time and energy mulling over something that clearly may not even have deserved that time. This brings us to the habitual worriers, those worry worms for whom worry is almost like a bad friend. They cannot let it go, but they know deep down that it is not doing them any good, and in fact may be very harmful to them. But, sometimes there can even be a pay-off for the worrier. They label themselves by saying that they are born worriers. They avoid taking risks. They can sometimes use worry as an excuse to be ill. They can use it to receive attention and some worriers may like the fact that they are seen to be more caring individuals. The down side of this is that they may be perceived as people who are not able to cope. They may be seen as neurotic or even hysterical. They may experience emotions ranging from anger, resentment, indecisiveness, self-pity and fear. These negative emotions in turn can prevent them from ever being free. They can be shackled to their worries and live their lives constantly worried about everything.

It is important to remember that, like a ship it is possible to lift anchor at any time and call to a new port and set down anchor there. The journey to the positive ports of this world may demand that you navigate many obstacles along the way. Remember to keep your eyes firmly fixed on your destination and try to focus on what you can do rather than what you cannot do. Stay away from negative forces or people that serve no other purpose but to bring you down. Try to keep in control of your own life, and recognise that any control you give away is a diminution of your own control and power. Think of new things and new experiences as a challenge, not a threat. List your fears so that you can get a clearer perspective on what it is that you are afraid of. Look at them from all angles, remembering that fear of failure can be someone else's disapproval or ridicule.

Emma is 24, attractive, lively, intelligent and fun to be with, but she does not think so. She spends her time worrying over what other people think of her and feels that no matter how nice she is to them, they will eventually end up disliking her and talking about her behind her back. Emma is now at the stage in her life that she almost invites disapproval by virtue of the fact that she always expects it.

Deirdre is terrified of speaking in public. Her fear can be traced back to the time when her teacher at school criticised her diction. This slight has stayed with Deirdre and she has long believes that not only can she not speak properly but that she is not much good at anything else. She does not seem to be able to rationalise situations and blows even the slightest suggestion out of all proportion. At other times she jumps to conclusions and makes judgements without sufficient evidence. This is having a very bad effect on Deirdre and her confidence is being eroded on a regular basis. In the long term this is applicable to anyone who is living in fear of bad things happening to them. and has damaging effects on their emotional, mental and physical well-being.

Our health is our most valuable possession and without it we are not free to do the things or go the places that we enjoy when well. To ensure that your physical well-being is in good shape, you need rest, exercise and good nourishing food. Equally, to ensure that your mental health it is important to sleep, relax, exercise and try not to take on more than you can. You wouldn't drive your car too hard or fill it with bad petrol, nor should you do so with your body. Listen to what your body is telling you. Heed the signals that tell you that you are driving yourself too hard and do not allow yourself to be caught up in mixed messages.

Consider Cormac. At the age of 30, he was one of the top lawyers in a thriving city centre practice. He worked extremely hard and was the first at his office in the morning and the last to leave at night. He always portrayed a healthy exterior. He talked often of the need to keep fit and look after one's health and he was a regular at one of the top gyms. When he started to get pains in his chest he refused to go to doctor and pleaded that he was too fit to be sick. He blithely ignored the warning signals and convinced himself that the pains were muscular as a result of his workouts. Nature eventually caught up with him and he had to be hospitalised. He was ordered to rest for three months suffering from burnout. None of us can afford to ignore the signs that tell them that we are going too far.

Our health is our wealth. Without it we are unable to cope or have the energy to think clearly, feel comfortable and do the many things that we may consider important. Do not be afraid to admit you have "low" days. This is the signal for you to take time out and restore your energy. We are all heading in the same direction, so it is up to each of us to do the best we can and grow old gracefully. Don't leave it too late and have others poking inside you, making decisions for you because you failed to look after yourself when you had the chance.

11. Sell-by date

What's the Hurry?

Stop. There is no need to hurry. Why do so many of us feel such a huge sense of urgency to get to the top, seal a deal or find a mate before it is too late. For many, life is like a fast race, always feeling that some one is out to catch us up, pass us out and reach the tape before us. Its almost as if each event in our life carries a sell-by date, or a sticker and unless a particular achievement is accomplished by a certain date there is a feeling that we may as well throw in the towel because our dreams and hopes will never be realised.

Very often, it is society that creates our own inner dates that determine the way we live. It is quite amazing to hear such things as: "so you never got married?", "you never had children?", "you're only buying your house now" said to people in their thirties, suggesting that if events are not achieved by a certain age that they never will. People can fell that they don't "measure up" when things like this are said to them. They can feel terribly inadequate if they haven't achieved all that others think they should by a certain time in their lives. They themselves may feel perfectly happy with the choices they have made, but it is a very strong and assured person indeed who doesn't feel second best to the high achievers who seem to have done everything. Life can be constantly evolving and exciting experience for all of us. Even those who seem to have it all, are often the very ones who feel as if they could be doing more. There is always time to do the things that you want to do, and setting a timeframe on this can mean that you don't allow yourself the freedom to enjoy the here and now. You may even look back on lost times or experiences with regret. Remember time regretted is time wasted.

There is only one sell-by date in our lives and that is our death.

There is no need to rush through everything and not to stop to enjoy what we have going for us at the moment. Chronologically we are all on the same route. Mentally, emotionally and physically, we differ. Depending on certain social issues, such as environment, finance, education and other external influences, good parenting usually lays the groundwork for the future development in our lives. Many people feel that they have to go along with the expectations of society and even limit themselves and their potential to fit in with this. They can go from school, to college, to marriage, to parenthood, to retirement, to death. Of course, life is only a bed of roses for the very few. The rest of us have to deal with the changes that life brings. Sometimes we have to struggle along to achieve our real potential with the nagging feeling that we are not performing to the best of our abilities. Indeed we may feel that we do not have what it takes to achieve anything that will be admired or recognised by others. However, we have the choices. We may have to make changes before we can make any progress. We need to be flexible, to accept the changes and to embrace the new possibilities that come our way. However, we must pave the way to make new decisions and changes as necessary, establish new commitments, new boundaries, and to move forward at our own pace, not at someone else's.

We can create our own transitional periods if we sense that there is a need for us to put our expectations on hold. We can relax, put things on hold and let things be for the time being. If we are to be constrained by the expectations of others, we can resent this and feel that they are living our lives. This can lead to feelings of resentment, dependency and vulnerability. Think of the woman who is being pressurised into having children without wanting them. Think of the woman who wants children, but because she doesn't have a man in her life, feels that time is running out on her. Men do not have that same pressure. Certain events can force us to where we are going. Sometimes, we need to change directions. The death of a relative can often make us stop and look at where we are going.

Many other things make us reflect on life; separations, ill

health, financial hardship, unemployment, success, and love
Some periods are times of great change, growth and upheaval,
while others are of relative stability where changes are consoli-
dated. Too many changes at any time can threaten our security,
while too little creates stagnation. There are some for whom
change is a time for rejoicing and challenge, while for others it
is a time that heralds fear and instability.

Emma is 38. She is not married and she is not in a relationship.
She desperately wants to have a baby and is terrified of facing
the future on her own. She really does believe that a woman is
not fulfilled until she has a child and she fears growing old
alone. She has recently been offered the chance to move abroad
with her job and though she has mulled over the possibilities
and opportunities that this may bring, she is terrified of taking
that first step towards making it happen for her.

Hostility towards ourselves often beckons when we reach
cross-roads in our lives and believe that we should be doing
more. The hostility may be both a protective and defensive
mechanism. It may protect us from taking dangerous and fool-
hardy risks but it may also shield us from the harsh reality of
truth. Some of us may also feel that the trouble it would take to
change is not worth it and we would rather sit back in perceived
comfort.

Louise is 53 and seems to have it all. She is very comfortable
financially. She lives in a beautiful home, has beautiful clothes
and jewellery and attends all the sought-after parties and
events. In reality Louise suffers the indignity of living with a
husband who controls her life so much that she even has to ask
him if she wants some money to buy a pair of tights. She has no
money of her own and is totally dependent on her husband. He
plays on her dependency and delights in making her feel that
she would be nobody without him. He seems to get a great
power trip from her pleading for money to buy the things she
needs. Her friends think that her life is a bed of roses and only
her children know what is really going on. Louise survives by
putting on a brave face. She has thought of leaving several times
but she feels there are many obstacles in her way. She is terrified

of her friends finding out that her life is in fact a sham and that her husband has so little respect for her. She is also afraid that she would not be able to cope on her own. Even though she has to beg for everything, at least she has it. In truth, Louise does not want to leave the outwardly comfortable life that she has. Even though she resents her husband's control over her life, she is more afraid of what she perceives to be the negative outcome of leaving. Though deep down Louise does believe that her life would be better, albeit in other ways if she left she is afraid of the consequences of change. If we have always been struggling to make it, we may need to pause and perhaps change lanes and find satisfaction in less material roles.

There is no doubt that political, social, cultural and economic affairs can influence our decision making. Sometimes financial dependence is a tie that holds a relationship together in the face of many forces that could pull them apart. Today the strain of transition from traditional to modern living can be difficult. Who would ever have thought when women were fighting to get rights for their fellow women that there would be such a backlash against feminism? Who would have thought that they would see a day that when men took on more responsibility for their children, that they would be seen as going against the grain and letting the so-called "macho" side down. Everybody, both men and women have had to change their expectations of their place in this world. Traditional living had more clear-cut roles for men and women. There was a simpler approach to life and living. Today, there are more options available which means more challenges to be faced and this gives rise to new emotional and mental pressures.

Modern influences make us question what we are doing and where we are going. Not only are we challenged to reach our potential, but we are also encouraged to express it. We are encouraged to express our individuality and assert ourselves. Today some people are rushing to take up assertiveness courses and go for counselling. There are many for whom doing course after course is just a habit. They are caught on the rollercoaster and don't know how to get off. Quality, not quantity is more beneficial at any stage.

Sinead is 49. She is well-off, has many friends but is deeply unhappy. When she worked as a model in her younger days she was used to admiration and being noticed. As the years rolled on she began to regret not studying for a qualification or doing other things with her life. She felt that she had relied too heavily on her physical appearance to the detriment of other areas. Sinead began to notice that as her looks faded, so did her personality and confidence. She decided in desperation to get a facelift. She genuinely believed that if her look improved, people's interest in her would be restored. However, the operation did not go as planned and Sinead was left with some scarring. She was terribly upset and seriously contemplated suicide. She felt as if she had tampered with nature and this was the price she had to pay. The sad thing is that Sinead felt that she had to look younger than her years. She felt that looks alone would be the key to a happy, contented and fulfilled self and believed that if everything was good on the outside, then all would be well on the inside.

Each era brings with it new challenges. We are now living in the age of ever-changing technology and telecommunications. There is no such thing as being to old to do something. Naturally, our age means that some of us do slow down physically, but mentally we can be as sharp as ever. We can limit ourselves unnecessarily if we just sit back and decide to do nothing just because the miles we have clocked up deem it proper to do so. There is a wonderful sense of satisfaction when we feel that we have done something that we always thought was beyond our reach. It could be going back to college at the age of 60. It could be learning to drive after years of being a passenger. It could be learning to paint, even though the art teacher at one stage threw you out of class. It could be travelling the world at 80. In fact, it could be anything at all and no matter what is it may bring you a wonderful sense of achievement. For some this can even open new doors. It is a great help if one can try and learn to see opportunities in events and experiences.

When a person is made redundant, it is a great shock that

often brings great worry and stress, but for others it can be a time of renewal and new chances. It could be the opportunity that you needed to pursue new avenues in life, explore new pursuits and maybe even follow a different career path. Life can take on a different meaning — no more routine, no more deadlines, no more targets, stress and strain. For others, the shock is too much to bear and they see redundancy and retirement as just that. They are retiring from the scene, retiring from life because they are redundant. They feel that their purpose in life is gone and n they have nothing to fill the void.

The suddenness can be too harsh, too real and can present psychological effects resulting in stress and illness. They may not have had time to plan and prepare the future and to get a clear idea of how to structure a new daily routine. There may also be fears lurking in the background that have to be addressed — fear of loneliness, of not being needed. They may also miss the camaraderie of working with a team and feel traumatised at being left on the outside. One also starts to question life itself and realise that the internal sell-by dates can be all mixed up.

In order to survive, you have to replace your losses with gains. Very often what you think is a loss is really a gain. Get going, get involved, get moving, start enjoying the here and now. Shake off any sell-by dates that are limiting you and hindering your ability to enjoy the one and only life that you will ever have. Life is not a rehearsal.

John, aged 48, was dreading reaching the half century mark. His perception of it was one of finality, old age, being useless and in some way being "finished". He felt so bad about the idea that his work and home life suffered. He lost confidence and at 49 he started an affair with a younger woman, flattered with the attention she was giving. Onlookers noticed his appearance and assumed he got over his recent bout of depression and was back on track. Little did they know that the new image was his last chance to relive the youth that he secretly yearned for and a way of avoiding facing the big 50.

When the younger woman left him, the shock brought him

to his senses and with professional help he realised all he could have lost. John was fortunate to reach his fiftieth birthday in the knowledge that instead of losing everything, he had time to see the light of day and was more aware of all he had — family, job and friends.

The bottom line for all of us is that we do not know our final sell-by date. We can only experience and enjoy life on a daily basis. Creating dates that have no foundation creates havoc. We can start by living life at our own pace — doing things that we feel comfortable with rather than doing something to fulfil another's ambition. Watch your own clock ticking not someone else's. You may be surprised to realise that the time is actually right. Remember, if you really want something it is never too late — so start now.

12. Side-lined or short-changed

Dealing with the blows

There are things in life that we are never prepared for. They come like a bolt out of the blue and really shake us up. They can make us feel as if life is definitely a trial and that we have been dealt a terrible blow. However, it is true to say that it's all relative. What may be a dreadful trauma or event for one person may be easier to take for somebody else. We all deal with things differently and we somehow stumble or struggle on. Some people seem to get it harder than most, but really no one ever escapes unscathed. We all have situations to deal with and events to get through. It may be the parents who discover that their child is gay, the spouse who discovers that their partner is having an affair, the person who is made redundant, the child who discovers that she has been adopted, the person who finds out that he has a terminal illness. The list is endless and we are all in there somewhere.

Whatever the sudden experience or situation, it can make us feel as if we are being cheated or short-changed in life and we may feel angry that something bad has happened to us. We may feel as if we are out of control and feel as if our expectations will never be realised. Very often the anger can be tied up in our own belief system being turned upside down.

For instance Hilda was a nun in an enclosed order. Eventually it dawned on her that this was not what she wanted to do with the rest of her life and after much soul-searching she left. Leaving was very difficult for her. She felt that she had put so much of her life into her vocation and that it was the correct choice for her. She now felt angry because she felt that she had been cheated in some way. On the other hand, Hilda's parents also feel as they have been short-changed. They see Hilda's decision to leave the convent as a waste of years of study and dedication, as if her decision was in some way a slight on them.

Peter left his wife for the woman he was having an affair with. At the time he was blissfully happy with his new love and things were going very well When their first baby came along, Peter felt as if some of the gloss was wiped off their relationship and he began to hanker for the carefree days when they were just a couple and did not have the responsibility of another human being. He has now begun to resent Barbara and even their baby and sees them as a burden. This was the very reason why he left his wife in the first place, because he was feeling trapped. He now feels as if his whole life is always going to be a disappointment.

Sandra married a man from North Africa. Her family feels as if she has put the whole family on the outside by her decision and they are all unable to cope with this. She can still recall the tension that surrounded her wedding and she looks back on this with extreme sadness and hurt. She feels on the outside looking in at her own family.

While non-acceptance can create further marginialisation however you also feel that your own predjuices and belief systems are being addressed. You feel that you are not going with the flow and part of you feels on the outside because someone is not conforming to your set of rules or values. In fact you feel sidelined for making a decision on your own.

Derek and Jane are like any happily married couple. They are very much in love and respect and care for each other deeply. Instead of being offered congratulations on the arrival of their first child, they have had to deal with the predjuice and resentments of those who most purport to love and care about Derek. Jane is Chinese and Derek's friends and family can't bring themselves to accept this fact. They think that Jane "is all wrong" for Derek and they don't want to be associated with the child as she is "half-caste".

Any issues that make us question can also make us look at what was our inner-core belief systems and this can leave us feeling very isolated. It may be the woman who marries a much older man, even though she always criticised those who did the same thing. It may be the man who marries a woman that his friends, or even he himself, consider to be less physically attractive than those he previously went out with or the person who seeks employment in an area that they once considered to be menial. On the surface many survive, even compensating change. Being a good student, day-dreaming about something, even rebelling are just some of the ways in which we can compensate when something in our lives is missing. These tools can help us feel content and repress feelings of rejection, isolation and loneliness and can choke our desires, wishes and dreams.

Sometimes years later we can awake and discover what has happened and try to make up for lost time. This can be apparent in the man or woman who has an affair, the rebellious adult, the person who feels that he or she has to chuck in their job and explore the world. Sometimes it is difficult to keep the lid on our fears and so we try hard never to let our guard down. It is almost like we are afraid to show our weak and vulnerable selves for fear of further isolation and marginalisation.

Children are often short-changed in life due to parents who don't have the ability to cope with their own turmoil. The child's vulnerability and neediness is often reflective of the parents' own feelings and they just can't come to terms with this. The parent who buries himself in a bottle or in working too hard and ignoring the child may be avoiding the responsibilities that parenthood brings. They may have many areas in their own lives that need to be resolved before they can recognise and cater for the child's needs and wants.

People are unable to help and support others if they can't help and support themselves. It is very important to realise that we sometimes bring about our own isolation by not reaching out, both inside and outside of ourselves. We must look inside to see if there is anything that we can do to stop the feelings of isolation and to try to separate feelings from reality. If you feel that you are being marginalised in some way, it is vital that you stop and assess this and make sure that you do something about it. No one has the right to isolate someone else and it may even take confrontation to sort things out.

Susan, recovering from a broken marriage and binge-drinking decides to venture back into the social scene of which she was once part. However, being sober, she soon realises that much of the chat she so enjoyed was through the haze of alcohol and now she feels very much sidelined. Gathering her thoughts, she realises that she was once part of this "outward show" and often left friends' houses not remembering what she said or what she heard. She is glad to be looking on, sober and having had the ability to deal with her own difficulties. She is comfortable in her own skin and welcomes the sideline. She no longer feels short-changed because she can give so much to herself and others with a clear mind.

You owe it to yourself to get the respect and the value that you deserve. If you don't resolve the feelings and the situations that isolate you, you will be forever stuck in the pit of despair and will eventually lose the will and the fight to do something to make you happy. If, however, you are happy and contented on the outside — good on you. You may have achieved what the rest of the world is searching for — a stress-free zone.

Create your own sanctuary. Like checking if the lights are out at night, check the demands made on you. How are they affecting you? Do they attack your body, thoughts or space. Act quickly when you get the attack warning. Take action and seek help. Very often we need support to alleviate the stress. Learn too from your mistakes. Look at the underlying causes and make an effort to sort this out. Go on give yourself a stress-free life.

13. Stress and Society

Reacting to the demands around you

We would all like to live an easy and carefree life. Some of us may even spend our lives day-dreaming about what life would be like without the daily dilemmas that interfere with this quest for happiness and ease. Think of the noise that a radio makes when it is not properly tuned. It crackles, hisses and interferes with our enjoyment. There are times when this crackling noise appears to get out of control and we have to switch it off. Our lives though are somewhat more complicated and we cannot reach for the off switch so easily. We end up stressed, tired and exhausted. This can be as true for the corporate executive as the harassed mother or the person beaten down by unemployment.

You feel as if you can't cope. You feel as if your life is out of control and feel as if you do not have the will to turn the tide. You may not recognise that you are under stress and you ignore the warnings. Think of that radio again and the noises that emanate from it when it is not properly tuned. It is signalling that something is wrong. Our bodies and our minds also make those same signals but we don't recognise them as readily as we do the objects that we have in our homes.

Everyone suffers from stress at sometime in their lives and even the happier moments in our lives can bring their own stresses — getting married, buying a home or bringing your first baby home. We seem to accept that the sad and turbulent times in our lives fill us with stress but fail to recognise that something doesn't have to be traumatic to be stressful. Equally, there is more help, advice and sympathy for the person who has lost his/her life partner, the person who has been mugged or made redundant than there is for the person who has moved into the dream home. It is right that there should be sympathy and understanding for those that have lost somebody or something, but it is just as important to realise that stress comes in many guises and for many reasons.

Today's society seems to be a breeding ground for stressful situations. There is so much competition, so many choices so many pressures. Some people thrive on this while others buckle under the strain. When the stress is exacerbated by other problems such as bad relationships, difficult bosses or colleagues, or sick children, the stressed person can feel under attack and some people can deal with this better than others. The real question that must be asked is why is it that some people can cope and others go under? This is often related to our perception of a situation, our ability to change and adapt, our ability to sustain difficulties and our ability to be strong.

Stress attacks us from three different sources: our environment, our thoughts and our physical being. This can include our job and domestic situations, our mental and emotional states and how we take care of our overall well-being. It is our own reactions to these threats that determine the amount of stress that we feel. We must observe what is really going on and decide when stress is building up. For instance, many people wake up in the morning and dread the day ahead. They may want to stay in the comfort and security of their beds and they feel very tired and lacking in energy.

Gemma is a typical example of this. She wakes in the morning after sleeping badly during the night. Her children clamber into her room, full of enthusiasm for the day ahead and demanding attention. The routine of sorting out lunches, schoolbags and all the children's needs do nothing to alleviate the stress that Gemma is under. As she works outside the home she also has to get herself ready and this adds to the tension. By the time she arrives at her office she feels like she has completed a day's work and is quite drained and lacking in energy. Gemma feels constantly in demand from one source or another and does not feel that there is any time just for her to relax and let things pass by. Gemma has been attacked by stress on all three levels: her physical being, as she is constantly rushing to get things going she does not have the time for breakfast and added to this is her lack of sleep and rest; her environment, lots of noise and heavy traffic en route to work; and lastly in her ability to deal with the stress in a measured and positive way.

Traumatic events in our lives can of course produce subtle changes that leave us feeling vulnerable, wounded and open to worry and stress. We can feel as though we are adrift like a tiny boat on a rough and stormy ocean. Of course there are people for whom worry and tension — stress — are almost like an addiction. They are habitual worriers and they can view life as if it was a great struggle and strain. They can feel daunted by the simplest things in life and find it almost impossible to relax and unwind. Even in old age the old feelings can re-emerge, particularly as thoughts of death come to mind, added to the loss of friends, and neighbours and failing health. Loneliness is a huge factor in enhancing and encouraging stress. At any stage in life; youth, adolescence, mid-life or old age, getting on the stress roller coaster is easy. The ingredients are all there, low self esteem, obstacles, inability to cope. Inability to change, fear, shame, being stuck in a rut. These are all the emotional symptoms and they can manifest themselves as burnout. Ridding yourself of these feelings is the real challenge.

First of all you have to acknowledge that stress is actually in your life. Have a chat with yourself and tell yourself that you are not comfortable with what is going on with you. Sometimes we may even have to resort to almost childlike instincts to set us on the road to recovery. Like a child we all need security, safety and energy to carry on. Being unhappy only makes us and those around us unproductive. Remember that you are the most important person in your life, and that you are more important than your own stress. Make a decision to conquer that stress and sit down and think hard about where it is coming from. Are you satisfied about what is happening for you?, if not, what can you do to change this. Are you happy in your job? If not, why not? Look at other careers and other opportunities? Are people in you life bringing you down and increasing your stress? If so, you need to address this. Make the people aware of the effects they are having on you and try to ensure that things change. What are your expectations? Sometimes we all need to look at why we want certain things in life and be open to explore different avenues.

Discuss the difficulties that you are having with the people that you trust and whose judgement you respect. Pace yourself so that you preserve your energy. Prepare yourself for likely repercussions. For example there may be people in your life who are causing a lot of the stress that you experience and once you try to change the power and the hold that they have over you may find that they are hostile to this change and they may even try to assert more control over you. Prioritise. Differentiate as to what is really important in you life. This can mean getting your home, work and relationships in order. Does it matter if the beds are not made in the morning, if the laundry is not done, if there is not haute cuisine for dinner? No! You could be getting yourself in a flap over things that really don't matter. Seek help if you feel that you really can't cope. For instance if you have lost a loved one, then don't be afraid to look for the help and the support that you need to bring back some peace, hope and joy into your life again.

Avoid letting anger and resentment build up and poison you. This only serves to blur your vision and eat you up inside. Discuss any conflicts that you may be experiencing. There could be conflicts of loyalty. For instance think of the conflicting loyalties that a person who is living a double life must feel. The man who is having an affair, on the one hand loyal to his wife and children and then loyal to the woman he is seeing secretly. Get into a clear frame of mind about how you want to be and try to picture yourself free of stress and anxiety. Honestly assess the pros and cons of any actions that you take in making adaptations. For instance it does take time to adjust to the changes in your life. Change your thinking. Make the transition easier for yourself, taking small steps initially and feeling comfortable with any risks that you need to take. Be prepared to change and break old habits and try to understand what are the underlying causes. Plan and make careful preparation. Practical, dogged and careful planning will eventually release you.

Remember to persist and have patience.

Relax and be honest with yourself. Tackle any addictions that seem to be blocking your path. We are all familiar with the person who drinks to beat the stress, only to end up with the drink beating him or her and the stress levels remaining and maybe even increasing. The habit that is most difficult to break usually stems from deep seated insecurity. What you must realise is that your safety net of drink, cigarettes, food is false and you are living in painful discomfort. How much longer are you prepared to fool yourself. Sometimes addictive people think that they are conning others, but the reality is that they are only conning themselves. Other factors come into play and bring more stress. Your relationships can be severely affected and children can suffer badly, as a stressful and anxious ground is being created for them.

Make life easy for yourself. Make your home a sanctuary, an oasis of calm, peace and harmony. It should be the place where you feel at one with yourself, safe and secure. Take time out to allow yourself to absorb your new energy and create new choices, new ideas, new goals no matter how simple that will allow you to live the life that you want to live.

When a person is wound up and stressed it can be quite usual for them to view people and their own lives in a totally different light. Little problems that once seemed as trivial as they de-served to be, can take on all the importance of ones that seem insurmountable. It can be common for people to become ob-sessed with the feeling that the whole world and all its people are against them and they can almost become paranoid.

Take Jack as an example. He was delighted to secure a new job and felt that he wanted to do better than anyone who held the position before him. He worked extremely hard and wanted to prove himself, not only to his peers, but also to his friends and family as well. Jack was by nature a perfectionist and he looked for and found flaws in his work. He became deeply unhappy at work and in his life. He imagined that people were gossiping about him and turning their backs on him and this added to the stress that he was under. He began to dread going in to work in the mornings and snapped at people with whom he normally got on well. He perceived them as being more successful than he and more competent. Naturally his work-mates took offence at this change in Jack's personality and they began to avoid him. Unfortunately Jack saw this as an endorsement of his feelings of suspicion about them and he became even more hostile to them. The situation became intolerable for him and culminated in Jack having a breakdown. It was only through admitting his difficulties and getting supportive therapy via his general practitioner and therapist that Jack learnt to enjoy life again.

Life is short. Enjoy it now. Recharge your batteries. Manage and organise your life to get the quality of life you so deserve. Don't have too high expectations and try also to enjoy the process of making your own stress-free haven.

14. What is your Role

Taking part or looking on?

Our entry into this world is often our first starring role. Some of us make a grand entrance, parents, family and siblings applauding our arrival. Others unfortunately are not so lucky and their entry is tarnished and unwelcome. Our roles throughout our lives are very often shaped by this first starring role. You can change many things in your life, but what you can't change are the circumstances that surround your entry into this world. Your next role in this life is to adapt to the world around you and realise and recognise that you are entitled to and deserve certain rights — the right to love, to care, to affection, to respect. It is a sad reality however that not every child is wanted and valued from the beginning. It may be the child who is handicapped, the child who is perceived as a mistake, the child who is born to single parents, the child who is born to mixed race parents or the child who is born as a result of rape. It is sad but true that these children are often made to feel as if they are not wanted right throughout their entire lives.

They sometimes get used to this and feel as if their very existence is a mistake and they carry this feeling with them through their lives and through their relationships. Sometimes the person who is unable to sustain relationships with lovers, family and friends alike, maybe was never valued and cherished as a small child. They end up feeling as if they do not deserve any love in adulthood. When we leave school or college, our roles change from dependency to independence and we see that we have to choose our own path in life. Some of us have difficulty during this time of transition and we may be fearful that we cannot cope. It may be moving out of home for the first time, it may be starting a job, it may be choosing to live in another country or getting married.

When you start your first job you may sometimes have difficulty fitting into your new role. It is a time of enormous challenge and uncertainty. Such basics as wearing a suit, getting accustomed to colleagues, dealing with authority and even trying to get on top of the work can all be difficult. We must try to learn and adapt. Then of course you have to get used to the reality that things do not always run smoothly and according to plan and you may even discover that you are in the wrong job and you may have to shake off one role and fit into another. Trial and error can often be required to find our most comfortable role.

Outside of your work you will also be placed in roles according to society's expectations and norms, family expectations and events. Should you choose to get married and have children you will be experiencing the role of parenthood. As we get older we usually fall into roles that are outside our control. We may fall into the role of a daughter, sister, brother wife, lover, husband. Some of us are allowed to enjoy and revel in these roles, while others do their best to run away The woman who is the apple of her father's eye may feel that this adoration is more than she wants and can cope with. She may respond by rebelling and try to get attention from others, in addition to her adoring father. There is also the woman who feels that her only role is that of mother and wife. She may feel as if she is being cast in a role not of her own making and may feel that other areas in her life are not fulfilled. The person who wants to change job to pursue other activities may not be able to do this because of their role as breadwinner. There are many instances in life where we see ourselves as tied to a role and wish to undo this tie. Sometimes you may find yourself in a situation where you do not feel that you belong or a role that you do not feel is right for you.

Fantasy may become a survival technique until you get an opportunity to make your dreams come true Of course some of us adapt to roles better than others and it is also true that there are many who bury themselves in their role. It might be the over-protective mother who cannot let go of her role. Some never get out of the role and extend it into their personal life —

the teacher who treats his or her children and friends as "little people" or the garda who trys to exercise authority over others outside working hours. Even in retirement, some people have trouble letting go of the role they held in their working lives as they still need the respect that their role may have given them.

Very often mixed messages occur for the onlookers who see the role of others in a particular way. It may be the person who discovers that the male doctor they respected belittles his wife, the garda they respected is crooked and not above corruption, that a journalist does not let truth get in the way of a good story. This can be devastating for the person who has put these roles and professions up on a pedestal. If and when they discover that the person that they revered has feet of clay, they can feel as if they have been cheated and may find it difficult to trust those in authority again.

There are, of course, many people who fall into a role that they are not comfortable with. This may be because the role does not fit in with their expectations and they may in fact end up resenting the road that they have chosen.

Maureen always thought that it would be nice to get married and have a house filled with children. When she got married at the age of 20, she and her husband decided to start a family as soon as possible and they had seven children in quick succession. Maureen's husband distanced himself from the responsibility of rearing his children by immersing himself in his work and all the responsibility has fallen to Maureen. She now feels as if a lot of her life has been wasted and tied up with childbirth, cleaning up, schoolrounds and the never-ending business of bringing up children. She feels angry that her husband has, in a sense, negated his role as a parent and that all the burden has been shoulderd by her. It is not uncommon for people like Maureen to see themselves in the role of a victim, always believing that life has dealt them a difficult hand. However, Maureen needs to communicate her concerns to her husband.

A role can be distorted by circumstances, poverty, illness and a lack of support. In a world where separations and divorce are common place it can be somewhat difficult for people to define their role. It can be difficult for the parent who is divorced and does not have the contact with the children that he or she would like to define their role. They may sometimes feel as if they are not parents in the sense that they and others understood and expected. The persons who are separated may feel as if they are in some kind of a twilight world. They can find it difficult to know how to introduce themselves to people they have just met, or indeed those they have not seen for many years.

Being separated or divorced can also raise other difficulties for people in a social environment. They may find themselves on the fringes of the couple set and feel that their presence is undesirable by the nature of their marital status. They may feel as if the couples don't really want to get involved with them as the couples are happy and in love and that anything different is in someway a threat or a blight on their happiness and stability. Equally they may be resented by one partner fearing that they may pose a danger and that they may be found attractive and desirable. It is not rare for many separated, divorced and widowed people to feel that they are not wanted in social settings. This can be very hurtful and isolating for them.

Sometimes even a person's appearance can slot them into a role that they do not want. If a person is attractive, dresses well and takes pride in how they look they may well find themselves in a role that has been created by society's expectations and images The woman who is beautiful, and sexy with brains, ideas and opinions to boot can nearly sometimes find herself cast in the role of the dumb blonde or the fiery siren. Many people would prefer to ignore that she is a human being, with all that that involves and place her in the role of the helpless, hapless and silly woman. This can be true of men and women alike. The man who is successful, ambitious and wealthy can often be pigeonholed in the role of the ruthless, heartless cold executive. People can forget that this man may be the kindest, warmest and giving of people. It is true that some people who are beautiful, intelligent, witty and imaginative can find that they have to work doubly hard to be accepted and for people to realise and acknowledge that they have many roles and not just the ones that are most obvious.

Roles can be very ambiguous and often people are not comfortable with that ambiguity. As explained earlier, there can be great status and power accorded to certain roles. There are individuals who will use their role to great effect. They can enjoy and revel in the attention that their role encourages and without this great sense of power these same individuals could crumble. Take the role away and the person feels naked and exposed and in some extreme cases, the person can suffer great stress, insecurity and illness if their role is taken from them.

Carol is 21 and eight years younger than her sister. When Miriam got married and had children, Carol was always quick to offer a hand to help her mind the children and baby-sit. Miriam and her husband Derek were able to go on enjoying a good social life due to Carol's kindness and her role as baby-sitter. However when she herself met and fell in love with a separated man, Miriam and Derek tried to put obstacles in her way instead of being delighted for her, pointing out that her new partner is separated and paying maintenance to his ex-wife and children. They pointed out so many barriers that Carol has second thoughts about her relationship and this resulted in petty arguments. Carol's sister and her husband thought that they were only looking out for her, not realising that family values have changed. They also forget that they met and married when they were both very young and without the benefit of being exposed to different relationships. They found it difficult to accept Carol's new role and lifestyle and in a way envied her new found personal life.

At certain times in our lives we have the chance to play out a role or wear a mask that can disguise us. Think of the popularity of masked balls, fancy dress and donning some fancy dress garb. There can be a great sense of freedom in adopting a different guise. This can make some normally insecure and unsure people feel as if they can do anything and be anything that they want. They can act out a role that is part of their fantasy with great gusto. In times like these we give ourselves the permission to be childlike, with all the wonder, expression and fun that a child enjoys and sees as his or her right. We can maybe think of the shy comic who wows the audience with hilarity and funny tales. He or she may be very reluctant to do this without the safety of the stage and the receptive audience. The comic may shudder at the thought of his or her true self being exposed and feel safe behind the facade.

Many of the roles that we adopt throughout our lives are protective and can shield us from the harsh blows of life. People who take on the role of the passive onlooker can be defending themselves from the realities of life, and though many others, not understanding this, may chide them for being weak and lacking in guts, the passive person may be using a very subtle form of protection. Take, for instance, the adult who was used to minding his parents and sacrificed their chance of outside employment to care for them and may find themselves redundant when the parents die. They then fall back into the only role that they have been used to, that of passivity or onlookers.

The same could be said of those who choose to stay in institutions. They are used to being cared for and protected and having others to make decisions for them. They may be terrified at the idea of trying to make it in the world on their own so they choose to remain on in the institution where they feel safe. Even those in certain work environments may shy away from thoughts of leaving as they feel that it is safer to stay put, in a job where their role is clearly marked, familiar and non-threatening.

Did you ever try on an item of clothing that did not fit? It may have been a dress that was too tight or shoes that pinched. Did you ever spend an evening in these restrictive clothes? How did you feel? I bet you were glad when the night was over and you could slip into something that did not constrict you. It might have been your shabby night-gown or your old, comfy slippers. Sadly, some people never take the opportunities to be comfortable cosy and happy and they eventually arrive at retirement with no energy left to embark on a journey of new discovery and experiences. They don't feel able to adopt another lifestyle. The energy has quite literally been drained from them. We should all aim for happiness in whatever role we choose and feel free to change and leave any role that infringes on our right to happiness.

We should be able to break off, fit in, move up, and move down to coincide with the changes that we want to see in our lives We all have those choices and it is up to us to make the changes that we want in our lives. Not easy for some, but always an option. We are after all, just passing through on this road. Nobody else is going to fight the battle for happiness for us. We have to seize the precious moments of joy and contentment for ourselves. Our lives are shaped by the roles we choose to fit into or not. We can switch roles even for a short time. We do not have to tie ourselves down and end up playing the role of the martyr throughout our entire life.

PART III:

THE COMFORTABLE SELF:
DETECT – CONNECT – PROTECT

15. Props

What are Yours?

In today's society therapy and counselling is paving the way for people to come out of the closet, so that they can have a clearer understanding of the problems that they have and where they can go from there. For many people who are trapped in their own worries and fears, lashing out at the world is sometimes the route that they take. They constantly feel weighed down by unhappiness and lash out at the wrong people. By taking responsibility for their own unhappiness they can make the decision to seek help and begin to see some light through the tangle that is around them. For some of course the idea of going for counselling can be seen as an admission of failure and they find it easier to go to the G.P.'s surgery pleading physical pain as the reason for the visit. The underlying reason is often so different, and they may omit to tell the doctor about the bereavement that they have recently suffered, or the loss of the long time lover or friend, or the loss of their job.

Ian was made redundant after 25 years in the same job. He was devastated, despite receiving a very healthy redundancy package. He felt a terrible sense of loss and felt that his whole security was very seriously undermined. He felt it almost impossible to deal with even the simplest of things that cropped up in his everyday life and was unable to absorb things because he felt totally dejected. This feeling of rejection carried through to his personal life and he began to imagine that those friends who meant a lot to him were in some way reluctant to be associated with him in the same way as before because they considered him to be a loser and this humiliated him further. He then suddenly began to feel very old and vulnerable as he perceived all around him were young people looking for work and he felt that all his contemporaries were comfortable and set up. Normally a man who was used to getting up early in the mornings, he began to stay in bed and felt listless and lethargic as he didn't see any reason for rising early. His family suffered and he was depressed and snappy and agitated.

Eventually, when his emotional torment manifested as physical pain he went along to the doctor, but he failed to mention his redundancy. The doctor detected that there was something else going on in his life and when pressed Ian poured out all the feelings of loss that he was experiencing. Even though he was initially loathe to go to the therapist that she recommended, he eventually began to see counselling as the prop that he needed to get through his troubles. He did start to see his life from a different perspective and realised that he was still young enough to begin something new and to explore other options. He also realised that he had enough financial resources to set up a small company which had been a silent dream. He recognised too that he had a lot of support from his wife, children and friends. Finally, he also saw that there are a lot of people in the same boat as himself and as a result he is more open and sensitive to their needs and feelings than he may previously have been. While redundancy was unexpected and painful the props that he used, therapist, further education and a new career move were the ones that he needed at the time. He also benefitted from getting a new outlook on life and he used his props to turn his situation around. We all need props from time to time in our lives and rather than pretend that we can get through things on our own, it is instead better to reach out for help and advice, and support ourselves from time to time.

Take Joe, the envy of his peers for his ability to climb the corporate ladder before he was 30. Joe also liked to prop others up and give a helping hand. When at the age of 40 he is sidelined for a younger executive he is devastated and practically falls apart. His pride is dented. He is no longer "top dog" and his confidence plummets. He isolates himself and refuses any help from his friends.

Eventually when he sees his children suffering he goes and listens to close friends who want to prop him up. Joe's props come in the form of willing to listen, take advice and change his negative thinking. He realises he has options. There is more to life than his job. He is fortunate to have friends who are there for him and are willing to help him.

Discovering you own props can be difficult particularly if you are weighed down by others. Consider Damian. At the age of 39, he has decided to come back to Ireland having gained enormous work experience abroad and to be there for his elderly parents living in the heart of the country. Initially he is glad to be back and able to help his parents at weekends, although he finds the weekly visits quite demanding. They both seek much attention and refuse home-help. Damian is torn between his demanding work schedule and looking after his parents. Having no siblings or wife, he feels quite isolated and dreads the country gossip and "isn't it about time you found yourself a wife". Damian hasn't the energy to look for a wife and indeed watching his parents bickering, he wonders if marriage is such a good idea after all. When his mother, after much persuasion, finally goes into a nursing home, he is still in conflict because he now has to go to the nursing home, look after his father at home and prop up both his parents. He becomes exhausted and when someone finally asks who props him up, he looks in disbelief. He feels guilty for having been abroad for so long and wonders how long his parents will have to endure their hardship. Both his parents are very independent and were always slow to accept help from outside the home. They believe it is Damian's duty to look after them. Damian is confused at his mixed feelings and it is not until he falls ill himself that he recognises the lack of support in his own life and the realisation that no one is there to care for him.

Props can also come in the form of disguised crutches that leave other people wondering about your new-found energy.

Celia is a teacher, lecturer and spiritual adviser to a large community. Everyone thought the world of her, admiring her stamina and ability to communicate so well. Celia had been living in a community of nuns and had always been happy in her role. When it was decided that the community would make modern changes, Celia became very anxious living in a two-up-two-down house with three other sisters plus wearing a more up to date habit became too much. Celia was terrified at the enormity of the changes and became very stressed. While being very confident and knowledgeable about her work, the coming-out from the veil was very daunting. Celia had difficulty sleeping and her mood dipped. However, she soon discovered mind-altering substances and sleeping pills that kept her propped up. Unfortunately, Celia found it hard to let go of these props and became addicted. While maintaining a strong external image, inside Celia herself knew the real message. It took years before she finally admitted the problem and sought help. Celia realised that while she was appearing to prop up her community, she in fact had no real support herself and used the pills as ways to survive her stressful and anxious lifestyle.

We can all use different methods to keep ourselves propped up and looking good in the eyes of those around us. Some of us become such experts that we become unaware of how our inner insecurities become disguised and vocalised as different messages.

Andrew works as a sales rep for a large multinational. While not climbing the corporate ladder as fast as he would like, he uses his family background to prop him up and intimidate others. Both his brothers and three sisters have professional careers and his parents are both doctors. Andrew however failed to get the required points for university. He felt deeply ashamed of this and feels he has ended up in a second-rate career. He compensates for this by going on about his professional background. He thinks others are impressed but in fact, they feel sorry for him as they listen to his designer talk.

We all use accessories to prop us up — designer labels, the latest fashions, gadgets, the right qualifications, neighbourhoods and holiday destinations. Initially, we get the thrill of being in the "right set" but at the end of the day, these accessories are only external and sometimes even shallow. We need to get to know the real self to give ourselves the correct props.

Consider Jane, married to John and working in a very demanding financial job. When their first child arrives, they are over the moon. However, when her maternity leave ends, Jane realises that her baby Jessica has to be minded. She finds it very difficult to find a suitable nanny and then John mentions leaving Jessica with his mother. Janes doesn't get on with her mother in law who is very possessive of her son. She feels reluctant to let her mind Jessica. Her dilemma causes her much conflict including a heated argument with John. When she finally agrees that she has no option, she allows her mother in law to prop her up but she is torn between feelings of guilt at leaving Jessica; gratitude to her mother in law; resentment at not being able to afford a top class nanny; and anger at having to work to top up a high mortgage which both Jane and John agreed to get a year ago.

She is being propped up but at a high price. She also feels she is using her mother in law, especially as she does not get on with her.

We must learn to be honest with oneself and admit when at certain times we need help or support. None of us are of any benefit to others, if we are filled with booze, pills or junk food to get through difficult periods.

Sometimes it is a matter of admitting defeat and realising our limitations are all too much if we need to be propped up. Do it NOW. It may be too late and you will never get to know the rejuvenated you.

16. Bound or blurred

Who binds or blurs you?

Think of a person who is bound. The word evokes feelings of constriction, lack of freedom and and unease. There are so many ways in which a person can be bound. It may be to a partner who is abusive, to a marriage that is dead and empty, to a friend because their presence only signifies safety and security, to a job that is not fulfilling in order to pay the mortgage and keep things going, by ideas of duty, to ideas that have lost their relevance and importance, to the past, to the future, dreaming that it is going to be better.

Niamh is a good example of one who feels duty bound. She is the youngest of a family of five, and all her brothers and sisters are married and living away from home. Four years ago, at 26 she wanted to leave the nest and get a place of her own but when she told her parents of her plans they were aghast and told her that she couldn't manage on her own. They also pointed out the cost of her decision, both in financial and emotional terms. They said that the financial strain would cripple her, rent, heat, food. They also said that she would be lonely on her own and would miss the company. All this negativity took its toll on Niamh and she decided to stay put. She is now 30 and the longing to strike out in her own is still there, but her parents are older now and the bind is tighter. When she attempts to tell them that she wants to move out they say that well she better off there with them and why on earth would she want to leave this nice, warm and comfortable home. The bind is now like a noose around Niamh's neck and she almost feels suffocated by her situation. She feels that her parents are coercing her to remain with them. She resents this very much. She feels as if they want her to stay, not as they say so that they can look after her, but instead that she can look after them as they get older. She is aware of their cosy set up and this annoys her.

Fear is the common reason why people stay bound to somebody or something. They are afraid to let the past go and let the future in. Fear blinds and blurs our thoughts and images. The expression "blinded by fear" or indeed "paralysed by fear" can root us to a spot where we feel secure and safe, even if this spot is bringing us down in many ways. Fear can be like a thief in the night. It steals our sense of adventure, our sense of freedom and our sense of strength. It can quite literally sap our energy and leave us feeling weak and fearful.

Alison is married to a man who spends more time at work and on the golf course that he does with her. She rarely sees him and is fully aware of the fact that much of his attention is also focused on a lady that he is romantically linked to and who also plays golf. As well as noticing the signs herself, Alison has also heard the whispers of his infidelity but she has chosen to ignore all this. She is deeply insecure and she sees her husband as providing a level of security that she does not have in herself. This is a false belief. She is blinded to the fact that by allowing her husband to compromise her by having an affair with somebody else he is eroding any little bit of confidence that she does have. Alison is bound by her own insecurity and also to her idea that marriage is forever, regardless of whether she is happy, respected and valued.

People can be also blinded by success and blurred by value systems. Many people think that having money, power and position gives them a license to treat others badly and they try to wield a power over those that they sense are subordinate to them. This is an attack on the dignity and uniqueness of others, but those for whom money is a God are blind to this. Equally there are the people who are blinded by money, power and position, and they feel that those who are privileged to have all this are somehow better than others. They may put these people up on a pedestal. Added to this people can be blinded by material success in that they feel envious of the advances of others and feel that they are inadequate. This can result in them being bound to an idea about themselves that is clearly undermining them and also prevents them seeing the very real talents and qualities that they have.

Tom works for a large insurance corporation. He is always available to lend a hand to others and can always be relied on to help out when a situation demands. Tom is actually blinded by the ambition of his work colleagues. He feels that he really cannot measure up and this is why he is always opting for the passive role. He is constantly being moved sidewards to accommodate the ambition of others and being blind to his own abilities has meant that he continues to feel second best.

Brian on the other hand heads up a top firm of property developers. He believes that he is entitled to the respect and admiration of those who work for him and he spends his time, wheeling and dealing with little respect for those who work for him. Brian thinks nothing of humiliating people in front of others for the smallest of mistakes and this seems to satisfy his need for power. Tom and Brian may seem to be poles apart but the reality is that they are both blinded and blurred by fear. Tom is blinded by his fear of moving forward and terrified of making mistakes along the way and Brian is blinded by his obsession with power and position. He would feel out of control without this and it terrifies him.

Friendship can bring a wonderful quality to all of our lives adding richness and warmth but when a friendship becomes a tie and has lost the mutual respect, spontaneity and consideration that is the base of a good and enduring relationship it may be time to reassess where it is going and how you want to deal with any problems that have raised their heads. For many people the ties of loyalty and familiarity are very strong and they can become lost in a world of memories and shared experiences which seem to shield them from the cold reality of where the friendship is at. Even though a friend may be treating you badly, you may have begun to take them for granted and even neglect and drag them down. Some people are just blinded by what used to be and they literally cannot see the woods from the trees.

Grainne and Sarah have been friends since schooldays and

have enjoyed much fun and laughter during the years. Lately however Sarah has been taking advantage of Grainne by borrowing money, clothes and CDs without bothering to return them. She has also stood Grainne up on a number of occasions and then used some flimsy excuse to wiggle out of her embarrassment. She seems to have lost all respect for her one time best friend and the sad thing is that Grainne is aware of this but because she suffers with low self esteem and needs friendship badly, she feels that she is better off with someone who treats her shabbily rather than be alone. Grainne is therefore not blind to her friend's selfishness, but she is bound and grounded by her lack of self esteem. This is in turn tying her to a liaison that is long since redundant.

If someone is lacking in confidence and self-assurance they can be tied to those who once boosted up their feelings of self esteem and this can almost be like a powerful magnet that draws them back time and time again. Then there are the people who are tied to the past, so much so that they cannot make the progression to the future and they are locked in a time warp. Even if the past has not always been so happy for them, the future may scare them more and they feel safer with what they know.

Terry wants to leave his girlfriend of five years. He knows that the romance is over. They have different opinions on a number of subjects, which instead of adding a spark to their relationship has the effect of causing many heated arguments which become bitter and personalised. He accepts that it would be better for both of them if they parted, However he has not been able to broach the subject with his girlfriend as he is afraid of the scene that would likely follow. More importantly, he dreads striking out on his own as he is afraid that he will never be able to recreate the magic and the fun that he and his girlfriend had at the start of their romance. He feels that even though this is now dead, the memories are still very much alive and he does not want to let them go.

Blurred and mixed messages are all around us in society. The man who tells a woman that he will leave her if she doesn't sleep with him and that she would if she really loved him; the employee who succeeds in getting employment in a company that has more to do with their connections rather than real talent; the employer who tells an employee that they are lucky to have the job that they have are mixed messages and examples of how the dignity and security of a person can be undermined. Boundaries are like the structures of a foundation. The boundaries surrounding a person's dignity and sense of belonging should not be compromised or manipulated by others who are trying to assert themselves at the expense of others.

Certain boundaries are important to maintain respect confidentiality and the dignity of the person eg doctor/patient relationship, solicitor/client. These boundaries keep us protected together with ensuring structure. Boundaries can give us a sense of how to move in the light of various situations.

Jennifer considers attending a conference with her new boss. She has a lively and vivacious personality that very often livens up dull and boring getherings. After only three months in the job, her boss needs her to impress the customers at this conference. Jennifer bumps into her former colleagues and ends up spending more time with them, swapping stories and indiscreetly giving business information away. Her boss is not very impressed and when they return to the office he has words with her. Jennifer had not been aware of her boundaries and loyalties to her present company.

It is important to observe boundaries, particularly in work situations where you can give and take information relative to your own profession. In most professions there is a code of ethics and individuals must adhere to these codes to maintain the standards of their own particular profession. If working for a large organisation or company it is common practice to stay loyal to information concerning the company while you are employed. If we were all running our own companies, we would like our staff to be loyal and respect confidentiality to our services. So stop, look and listen when you are giving away information. Some day you may be sorry you let the "cat out of the bag" and some else has pinched your clients. Because we live in such a competitive world people are always waiting to jump in to our shoes. Boundaries ensures security and ultimately stability.

17. Stand up and be counted

Who is taking the stand?

Stand up for yourself, Richie's mother screams when she hears that he has let somebody walk all over him. Unfortunately Richie does not understand what "stand up for yourself" means. Because he is so vulnerable at present he is afraid to admit that he doesn't know what this means for fear of further reproach. He is ten and he thinks that he is meant to be a big boy and big boys don't cry. The other side of this is that Richie has never seen anybody stand up for themselves. His mother does not stand up for herself when his father shouts at her about things that are seemingly trivial. Richie is confused. He understands words, but does not grasp the messages behind them. Intonation, sarcasm, body language, interpretation are all lost on him. This may be due to two things. First the fact he is too young to decipher all of life's codes and secondly he may find the whole concept very grey. For instance, he knows that he should stand up when the teacher walks into the class. He believes that this is a sign of respect. He also knows that he should stand aside for elderly people to walk ahead of him. He should stand back to let somebody else pass by in the street, but as for standing up for himself, he just doesn't understand.

Sometimes when people are over-protected and shielded from making any mistakes they may find it very difficult to stand up for themselves when things and people go against them. This in turn can lead to a vicious circle as they may feel more and more open to attack each time yet less able to defend themselves from further onslaught. They are not used to confrontation and do not have the necessary tactics to deal with it. They may eventually become extremely vulnerable and this in itself may frighten and confuse them. Like Richie who has to learn how to break free from his fear and timidity, adults must learn how to take more control of their lives and learn to defend themselves assertively, rather than aggressively. Those who have children must become conscious of how they behave in front of them as they can often send out a multitude of mixed messages to children. Children feel secure in the knowledge that their parents are in control in a non-aggressive and non-threatening way. Parents cannot expect their children to be assertive and in command when they are sending out mixed and different messages to them all the time. Children who are not listened to, nor understood and who are experiencing pain and distress can be affected for the rest of their lives.

Niall has always lived with a fear of his father. His mother used to hold him up as a threat when she was unable to deal with Niall in a firm but loving manner. "Just you wait until your father gets home" was the constant message that the child was given. As a result, his father was seen as somebody to be afraid of and this stifled any chance that Niall would have had to establish a loving relationship with his father. In a sense, Niall's mother was using her husband as a means to avoid chastising the child. She was afraid to stand up for herself and this resulted in further conflict for Niall and a host of mixed messages bombarding him daily. The first being that his father was somebody to be feared and secondly that his mother did not have the authority to resolve issues with her child on her own.

Patrick excelled in his academic work at school, but he had little or no interest in sports. His father was one of the country's sporting greats and he wanted his only son to take up his football boots. Because the child did not have the interest in and love for football, he did not make the team and rather than stand up for himself and declare his non-interest he struggled on. He was the target of the scorn and derision of his sporting competitors. Instead of trying to assert himself he carried on and took on board a lot of hurtful comments. His father's disappointment with him increased his sense of powerlessness and even his schoolwork, which he had always loved, began to suffer. Patrick is now 16 and has little or no confidence in himself. He has shied away from making friends with others of his own age and he spends much of his time alone. Because of his father's harsh attitude towards him which included ignoring him and ridiculing his lack of sporting prowess and finally rejecting him, Patrick became very depressed, and attempted suicide. When his parents discovered this, they immediately became concerned and wondered where they had gone wrong. His mother blamed his father and vice versa and the ensuing merry-go-round of criticism and counter-criticism did nothing to help Patrick's sense of inadequacy.

Basically, Patrick had been listening to mixed messages: to achieve, but only on the football pitch; to get to the top, but only kicking a football; and to be as good as your footballing father. Nobody ever helped Patrick to develop his own talents. His father denigrated his academic interests and never acknowledged that they were important. When Patrick finally succeeded in getting help, he spilled all this out and also told of the times that he had been bullied by those who said that he was stupid because he couldn't kick a ball properly or score goals. It is important that parents take a stand on issues of how their children are treated, rather than hoping that somebody will understand and respect their dignity, be they a teacher, a scout leader or a coach. When parents take a stand, they invariably instil a sense of security and strength in their children, who will be less likely to be targeted, singled out or picked on by other people. This sense of strength will carry them through to adulthood and will be invaluable in helping them to deal with the many issues that arise.

Some people who have been passive allowing things to carry on without their input, while seething quietly inside, blossom in their late twenties and thirties. This is because they finally learn how to stand up for themselves. They begin to see the difference between passive, aggressive and assertive behaviour. They can interpret what is going on around them. They begin to detect the people who are out to bring them down. They begin to see that they have rights as human beings and that nobody else should take the power, and equally be given the power to hurt them. They begin to stand up for themselves. For some, the support of a group can be invaluable where they are given the courage to stand up and be counted. They then begin to become aware of their own standards, the standards of others, the standards that have no value and they discover ultimately what happens when they break their own standards.

Remember that life is short and you have the right to be happy and be counted. Do not be on standby for the flight to happiness and serenity. It is here in this life, in this existence for you to enjoy, so spread your wings and stand up for whatever you want. Finally if you do not stand for something, you could fall for anything.

18. Watch your step

Are you looking behind?

One small step for man, one giant step for mankind. Many of us felt the amazing sense of bewilderment when we watched Neil Armstrong succeed in his ambition to be the first man on the moon. We never imagined it possible for man to accomplish this wonderful feat. Many people will never have the chance to achieve the things that are heralded as successes and instead they may have to settle for watching others take the applause. This can be in every strata of life, and for many people, the first step that has any significance for them is watching their children take their first small step.

For most parents, the birth of a child is a cause of much jubilation and happiness and they will watch proudly and indulgently as the little one takes their first step. Sadly however, this is denied to some people. They may have a child who is disabled and may not be able to walk. Their cherished child may die before he or she ever gets the opportunity to walk and equally some people may not be able to have children and this can be the source of much sorrow and pain.

John and Imelda are both in their early thirties. They both work and do not have any financial worries. During the first years of their marriage they waited patiently and excitedly for the birth of their first baby. Both their parents and extended families also shared their anticipation. Unfortunately this was not to be and they have now come to terms with the fact that they will never be parents. The realisation is so painful for them that they find this very difficult to talk about. They are also faced with the pressures from their parents and others who continuously ask them when they can expect to hear the patter of tiny feet. They see this as a gross intrusion into their lives and sometimes feel as if the people who ask them about babies are even trampling on their pain. They are also aware that some people think that their childlessness is by choice and that they are envied. Some of their friends believe that their cosy set up is all that really matters to them.

What mixed messages they receive. Some even make comments 'that it's well for them not having children to tie them down'. Sadly all of this pressure is getting to John and Imelda and their relationship has begun to suffer. No money in the world, or success at work can give them the one thing that they really crave, their own child. Even their efforts to adopt a child are met with obstacles as Imelda is told that she is too old, at 37. Difficulties also arise when they tried to go further and secure a foreign adoption. John and Imelda may have to step outside their feelings for a baby in order to hold on to their own relationship. It is only when they learn to accept their situation, meet other people who are in the same boat that they can begin to step out of their own turmoil and start to be more at ease. Infertility can be very painful for people, even more so in a society that views couples with children as the norm. In all types of relationships, we have to be aware of the sensitivities of others and the importance of avoiding stepping on somebody's toes.

Take Fergus for example who is young, dynamic and ambitious and can't wait to climb to the top of the corporate ladder. Unfortunately this may not become a reality for Fergus in the company where he presently works as he has stepped on his bosses' toes once too often. Subsequently a very tense atmosphere has developed. Fergus has not learned how to step back and observe what is really going on in the company, like who is reporting to whom, who are friends and who are not. He has not learned that there is a time and a place for everything, including certain comments. If Fergus decided to step back and look at where he is going wrong, he may realise that he can lead a much happier and trouble-free life if he has consideration for the feelings of others.

As a society we need to become conscious of the people who are forced into situations that are not of their making, the mother whose son is a drug addict, the father whose son is in jail or the daughter whose mother is an alcoholic. The examples are many, but it is important to take note of the feelings of people connected with those who are perhaps ridiculed, marginalised or maybe even feared in society. They may equally feel their pain and it is important that other people do not add to it and make bad situations worse. While some people may feel that they have stepped outside a situation, others may feel that they have stepped in, particularly in relationships. A common mistake that some people make during the early stages of a relationship is to divulge issues that are probably best kept for later, when both people have had the chance to get to know one another. For some, this need to spill everything out quickly may be spurred on by a desire for closeness. Of course closeness is vital for the growth of the couple, but other people might not be ready for such intimacy and they may be frightened off. Equally there are people who may confuse the role of their partner and see him or her as some sort of a counsellor or therapist.

They may see the new partner as someone who can solve all their problems and they can then feel very hurt, let down and disillusioned when they realise that their partner is just that, a partner and not somebody who possesses any special powers to ease away worries and fears. They don't have any magic formulas. They are after all just human. To expect them to be anything else is unfair. It can be very confusing, not to mention almost frightening for someone to find themselves in the position of pseudo-counsellor. They may accept that relationships are all about sharing, but they may also feel that things are being dumped on them too quickly and they just may feel unable to deal with this so early in a relationship. Sometimes we may have to take two steps backward before we can take one step forward.

Alice is happily married with two children. She works outside the home and loves her job but she has her sights set on promotion. This involves doing a course to update her skills and after much deliberation, Alice has decided to do the course. However the pressure of working, studying and looking after her home and her family is building up for her and she is suffering from exhaustion. When her exams were looming recently, she panicked and was convinced that she would fail and got herself into a terrible state of worry and anxiety. She passed but her relationship with her children and husband suffered badly.

What Alice needed to do was to take two steps backward, in order to move forward. It was great that she wanted to better herself and do the course, but she would have saved herself a lot of trouble if she had cut down a little on her workload, cut down on her family commitments and postponed her exams. Alice needed rest and relaxation and then the experience of studying for the promotion would have been happy and one to look back on with good memories.

Other people who are also striving to be the top dog sometimes realise that to step down and accept a lighter workload is the answer to solving the problems of stress, worry and exhaustion. Stepping down from something can be a very courageous step, especially if you have been involved with a company or organisation for a considerable length of time. Though it may initially be a terrible wrench, it can also lead to a wonderful sense of freedom and relaxation.

Whether you step up, step down, step in, step out, the main thing to remember is to do it all one step at a time. Living one step at a time sounds rational and logical, but very often confusing for the person who spends his time projecting to the future — some even live so far ahead that they wonder who will turn up at their funeral.

Brenda is anxious about her holiday abroad with her colleague Angela. At night, she tries to live out the future holiday, wondering will Angela and herself get along. By the time the holiday arrives, she is almost worn out and cannot share Angela's enthusiasm and this puts a damper on what should be fun time.

Projecting to the future is almost a daily chore for some. They worry about events that have not occurred. They even take on worries that they have no control over and can end up upsetting others.

Marjorie's son Tom is studying for the leaving certificate . She is terrified he may not achieve the points required for his chosen career. She stresses herself out worrying that he might not be successful. Tom, himself is very laid back. He refuses to get hooked into his mother's worry and this has in fact upset her more. She fails to see Tom's philosophical and relaxed attitude to life and constantly urges him on. Fortunately Tom is gifted with a very relaxed and happy personality together with an informed mind and an ability to work at his own pace. He realises you can only do one subject at a time and with those hours you can only achieve your best efforts. Looking behind wastes time and looking forward uses up unnecessary energy. When Tom finally completes his exam and gets the required points, Marjorie realises how worn out she is and how she did not trust Tom. Instead of watching him all the time she realises it's her own steps she needs to watch. Very often we have the answers to others' problems and fail to see our own situations.

While we once needed someone to teach us our first steps we should now be able to step it out in style, provided of course we avoid stepping on others' toes, stepping out of line and getting our steps all mixed up.

19. Veiled threats

Whose voice?

The image of a veil conjures up images of little girls on their first holy communion days or older girls on their wedding days. Then of course there are the veils that are worn by women in Islamic societies. Some are shrouded in black to conform to their Islamic customs, and want to shield themselves from the curious eyes of male admirers. This of course can be quite confusing for western society, particularly in an age when women are making great advances towards equality. The image of a veil conjures up a picture of something that is being hidden. It can be used as a disguise. There is a sense of mystery that actually seduces and invites. The part that is covered leaves a lot to the imagination, an imagination that can often run riot. There is enough peeping through to whet the appetite for more.

Sometimes in our relationships the notion of a veil can come into play in the form of a veiled threat and in this context the word "veil" can be used for protection, not for those that they are hurled at, rather more to protect the person who is aiming them. It is like they want to cover up the ugliness of their threats and wanting the recipient to only get a "peep through" message. A veiled threat is like a covert warning of intent to do harm, but sometimes the person who is being threatened in this way may find it difficult to decipher what is really behind the message. This is one of the most insidious issues about veiled threats. The person who uses them is actually keeping the other person under their thumb as they may never be really sure what is going on. The antagonist may portray an image of one who is nice, understanding and genuine, but behind all this are the constant undercurrents of the threats.

Linda and Nuala have been friends for years and share a lot in common experiences. But for most of their friendship Linda has been wary of and insecure about Nuala and wonders whether she has any real loyalty and affection for her. Whenever there is the slightest ripple of unease or strain in their friendship Nuala churns out the veiled threats to abandon Linda. They are very subtle, but cut to the quick as she says that she is getting bored with her life and feels that she needs to do more things and meet more people — threatening Linda's place in her life. Of course, she is actually damaging their friendship as she has shaken Linda so many times in the past to the point where the girl has asked herself many times what she is doing with a so-called friend who sets out to threaten her. Linda fails to confront the issues for fear of total rejection.

Killian is the eldest of five children. When he was twelve, his father left his mother, who had to bring up the family single-handedly. However, she relied heavily on Killian despite his tender years and brought him into a world that he was far too young to understand. She would constantly use veiled threats when she said that the children are all she had, and if anything happened to them she wouldn't know how to cope. His mother was keeping the children under her thumb as she didn't have the necessary skills to deal with them properly. She herself felt threatened by them, by their happiness and exuberance and guilty at their being neglected by their father. Of course what she did then was to erode the confidence of her children, particularly Killian as he was the eldest and he had to bear the brunt of her insecurity. Killian felt that he had to protect his mother whereas it was he who needed the protection, the support and parenting that his mother couldn't give him and which his father had neglected. This experience in his early life has left Killian over-anxious and nervous. Even now, as a married man with a family of his own he still feels the pangs of insecurity and has to fight a constant battle not to over protect his children in compensation for his own lack of parenting.

Threats are often even more difficult to deal with when they come from people who once meant a lot and sometimes we may even wonder what we did to deserve the veiled threat. In relationships that are going stale, the person who wants to get out may use a form of a veiled threat instead of actually confronting and being honest with the other person, hoping that they will get the hint. They do not seem to have the courage of their convictions. One of the most common forms of veiled threats are made by parents who threaten to cut their children out of their will if they don't toe the line. Equally, veiled threats can be used by employers.

Alanna is the boss of a medium sized computer company. She is a difficult woman to work with at the best of times and is given to flights of temper. She tries to assert her own authority by making her employees feel insecure. She does this by constantly telling them how difficult it is to find work these days and that they are lucky to be in a job. The veiled threat is that she can fire them if she wants and also gives her a better sense of importance.

Veiled threats are common in the case of failed love affairs when the common cry may be "if you leave me I'll killl myself", or in the case of an extra-marital affair, "if you leave me I'll tell your wife/husband".

Veiled threats and veiled insults can also come in the form of carefully chosen words of praise for former colleagues, friends, lovers and employees. These can be extremely subtle and are entirely different from the recognition that should be given to people deservedly. . . .

"Everyone was mad about Aisling. She was full of fun, but people will get used to you in the end. It is just that it can take time for them to adjust to new people in the company." or

"Nobody has ever understood me as well as Janet did, I felt as if the two of us were soul mates and meant to be together for the rest of our lives. She was out on her own really."

People can use threats in the same way that they use power. They use and manipulate their words and messages to drive home the belief that they are in control, that people should hold them in awe, admiration, and view them with respect. Of course the people who feel the need to bully and force their opinions, needs and wants on to others are usually weak, troubled and insecure.

Catherine, who is 78, has no one person that she considers to be a faithful and loving friend to her. She believes that people are only willing to spend time with her when she is willing to spend money on them. Her brothers and sisters did not do as well materially in life as she did, but she envies them their sense of fun and humour. As a result of this she tries to lord it over them and is always ready to point out that the clothes that she wears cost a lot of money, the furniture in her plush apartment is the best that money can buy and that the hotel she stayed in whilst on holidays was the best and most expensive in the whole resort. Catherine is deeply jealous and resentful of her family and she feels that the only way that she can gain any respect or recognition from them is to promise that they will be looked after in her will. Of course this is not a gesture of generosity and peace. Instead it is meant to make her family believe that she is special by virtue of having money. Of course, when things are not going Catherine's way and when she is upset at some small family misunderstanding she takes to threatening her family that she will cut them out of her will. This is done very subtly, but the message remains the same, that is if they don't toe the line as she sees fit they will have to do without her money.

Threats of any description are hurtful for the recipient. They can create havoc in someone's life, particularly if the person hurling them is anonymous. Joan was plagued by anonymous phone calls which threatened her security. Living on her own she became very nervous and finally had to change her telephone number.

Veiled threats are equally disturbing and thougt there may not actually be any intention of taking action, the recipient, nonetheless, feels the sting and it can be very emotionally draining. Threats of any kind should be dealt with immediately, before the situation gets out of hand. Individuals need to protect themselves from future onslaughts and confront the threat instantly. If you are nervous about future victimisation, seek help, professional or otherwise.

You have to learn to protect yourself from any sort of subtle abuse. Nowadays, our telecommunications system can protect clients to ensure security. Don't leave yourself open to disturbed people who are often a menace to society.

Jean was on her way home from work when she was almost attacked and mugged. The would-be muggers jeered and hurled threats at her before they finally attempted to hurl themselves at her. Fortunately Jean was carrying a personal alarm and let it off just in time to scare the menaces away. From experience Jean has learnt to protect herself at all levels. None of us can ever be to careful. Your own veil should cover you in comfort and security.

Don't let threats consume your life. Allow them to disintegrate like going through a sieve and suss out what is really behind the threat flung at you.

20. Get real — Get a life

Who gets what?

"Get real" screams 15-year-old Jason to his parents. Unfortunately his parents don't understand the modern day lingo and they retort back defensively and tell their son that he should grow up. Jason's parents have forgotten that he is just going through the process of growing up. They too had to go through that same often turbulent, uncertain and perhaps even painful process, though the memories of that may have faded for them. Jason's parents are now in their fifties and they find it difficult to accept that their once placid, calm and easy-going son is proving difficult to handle. They are finding it tough to be challenged on subjects that seem to be flung on them with increasing consistency. Formerly taboo subjects are being raised in their household. They find the questions, strange, even frightening. In fact Jason's idea of "get real" speaks as a real threat to his parents who are living a life that they hope their offspring will imitate. Instead of listening to Jason and trying to explore the issues that he is trying to grapple with, they try to cope by literally shutting him off.

Jason feels embittered and confused. He wants answers and not the mixed messages that his parents persist in sending him. On the one hand they are telling him to grow up, on the other they are telling him that he is not old enough to be privy to the kind of information that he wants. In fact Jason is hungry for knowledge and he is at a cross-roads between listening to his peers talk about idealism and trying to fight the grown-up battle. His parents are always putting him down and are terrified to actually stop and really listen to him. There are many things that he wishes his parents would help him with. Instead they seem intent on pushing him into things that they themselves did not have to do. For instance, he is all at sea about his parents' lifestyle which is enviable. They seem to have it all and yet they did not go through the college system. They were supported in every way by their parents, and have never known unemployment, poverty or exclusion.

On the other hand Jason does not feel that he has this same support and he is worried about the future — will he get a good leaving, the chance to go to college, secure a good job and enjoy all the trappings that his parents do?. Jason feels out in the cold. He tries to be grown up, but very often he feels very lost and lonely. His older brother is studying in England and his parents are seldom at home. When he says "you don't understand me" he means it, but his parents interpret this as the emotional turmoil that they believe all teenagers go through. They think that he is all mixed up and that he will grow out of his rebellious ways. When he becomes quiet and somewhat tired of the battles, they immediately suspect girl problems. When he is out with his friends and is late home they fear that he is mixing with the wrong crowd. Drink, drugs, crime and sex are the images that come into their heads. It is sad to see what has the potential to be a loving, secure and mutually respectful relationship between Jason and his parents turn into a battle ground. Things could be so very different if Jason was given the attention and tolerance that he needs.

Generally all parents like to think that they are in charge of their brood and that they want to impart to them their value systems. Real values and responsibility are all about being the key-holder for one's own power and control. Knowledge gives information which in turn gives confidence to children who learn about tolerance and respect. Parents who command respect are seldom those who throw out mixed messages and falsehoods. The parents who do command respect are the ones who lead by example and don't react thoughtlessly. The E words — education, experience, effort and energy — can be applied to both parents and their children. Teenagers, in particular thirst for information and answers. Some parents might score higher points on experience, but lack the same level of formal education. Of course it is often this same experience that sometimes leads parents to chide and reprimand their children, because contrary to what teenagers may think, parents do know what it is like to be young and to have all the restlessness and energy that goes along with being young. Parents must put effort into their children by giving them time, support and love.

They are also familiar with the antics that young people get up to so it is no surprise that they can fret and worry. They have been there. But it is not enough for parents to give out and not give the reasons for their disquiet. The mixed messages can be bandied about. They may tell the teenagers that they are too young to go out and then in the next breath tell them they should cop on to themselves and start acting their age. Then of course some teenagers see their parents in no hurry to grow up themselves as they trot off to the gym, the beauty salon and the health gurus in search of the fountain of eternal youth. What a contradiction this can be and no wonder that teenagers are confused. The journey through adolescence is like a journey to Mars, wonderfully exciting, challenging and often scary, even nerve-wracking. Deep down teenagers do like and need to know that they are being supported. They need the unconditional love of parents who boost them up and give them confidence in an uncertain time. They most definitely don't want to be compared with others who may appear better behaved. This can only serve to confuse them and give out the mixed message that they can only be cherished and a source of pride when they are behaving in the way that their parents want them to.

Claire and Donal lead a very active social life. Fortunately their eldest boy Niall who is 17 baby-sits his younger brother Tony who is 10. They are delighted that they have the freedom to go out with other couples knowing that Tony is looked after. They are happy in the knowledge that Niall is watching videos, eating pizza and that Tony goes to bed at 8.30. Little do they realise that Tony is in fact watching videos with Niall until past midnight. Sometimes the videos have sex and violence in them which Niall finds absorbing and forgets Tony is with him. Claire and Donal wonder why Tony has become cheeky and blame his schoolmates for the new verbal outbursts. Niall feels it is not his responsibility to bring up Tony so never mentions the late-night movies.

There is also the mixed message whan a parent has an affair. There can be all sorts of confused ideas floating in the teenager's head. What do you do when you find out? Who do you tell? If it is your father does your mother know? Do you just pray he gets over his little fling? Are your parent's going to break up? The bottom line is how do I cope? Very often young people are caught in the middle between mother and father when there is an affair taking place. The crisis can come to a head not only between partners but also parents and children. Sometimes the childfeels he/she is acting the parent when they their parent getting all excited and dressed up to go on a 'date'. The difficulty for the child is that he/she may end up saying: "Don't be out late"! What a mixed message. The teenage years are trying enough without the hazard of protecting your parents from their crazy set ups. Parents must stand back and look at what is really going on and avoid their children becoming old before their time. Infidelity, betrayal and flings can have long term damaging effects and sometimes it is too late to turn the clock back.

Of course these mixed messages are not confined to the family homes of Ireland. They are all around us and sometimes we can feel as if we are in a minefield, so it can be very difficult to determine what message we should really take. For instance we may work hard and do our best to pay all our taxes and do everything above board and then we hear about those in positions of power who are involved in all sorts of scams. We may be told by the church that sex before marriage is wrong only to discover that the parish priest has fathered a child. Equally we may be told by that same church that abortion is evil and then find out that a member of a religious order has tried to pursuade his lover to abort their unborn child. We may be told that it is wrong to be unfaithful to a spouse only to find out that those that we held in admiration think nothing of having the odd dalliance, but the sin is in getting caught.

Mixed messages not only confuse but leaves us all a little

mixed- up. Maybe we need to all "get real" and learn to detect the real message, protect ourselves with real support and connect to the real world and the real self.

21. Mixed messages, Mixed emotions and Mixed ideas

Who is really Mixed Up?

Isn't it wonderful in today's society that we have so many different forms of communication. In fact we can take much of it for granted. Just think of the forms of communication that we have at out fingertips — the telephone, the answering machine, the mobile phone, the fax machine, the internet, the voice mail and the bleeper. These advances have no doubt, made life easier for many of us, but there are the others who do not have the same trust in the new modern gadgets and they feel safer with the old school.

They feel that people can be too dependent on technology and they wonder what would happen if all the modern fandangled things broke down. Who would be to blame? Who would take the rap and what if the messages got mixed up? The television and the radio for long were the sources that people relied on for their picture on the wider world and of course still do to a large extent. The television screen that beams into our homes brings us messages from all over the globe, from Asia to Artane, from New Zealand to Newbridge, from China to Cork. We can receive, via the transmitter, the message that someone wants to send us. However there is sometimes a complicated mix of factors that can leave us confused, questioning the world in a different light as we approach the new millennium.

Politics, sex, religion, economics, social issues all leave us thirsting for more answers. We know that we must distribute wealth, but yet images of mega-rich tycoons flitting around the world can fill our screens; Men and women are getting together, even though they are married to other people; the champions of the poor dressed in expensive clothes and travelling first class in their journeys to tell the world of the agony of those on whose behalf they claim to speak. Without having to leave the comfort of our armchairs we are catapulted into the world created by imaginative writers and producers.

Sometimes, however the cameras can miss the big picture. While we zone in on the complicated legal, social and economic information from all over the world, at other times our lens need readjusting and we continue to miss the big picture. It is easy to blame the media, the newscaster, the politicians and anybody else who may spring to mind for the fact that the stories that we are listening to are ones we do not want to hear. Added to this is the fact that we ourselves continue to mix up the messages. The unravelling of the mixed and complicated messages lies within our own being. While we can sometimes veil the issues and get by without questioning, this can lead to a distortion of the facts.

There comes a time when we have to step back and look at the method behind the madness, the issues behind the glib statements and the truth behind the mixed messages. We can of course choose to live the life of the armchair critic. We can choose to be the person who doesn't budge, but is begrudging of everybody and everything. We can choose to be the people who judge, without bothering to familiarise our selves with the reasons for our bigotry. We can choose to see the unhappiness and isolation of others without ever wondering, even in passing, what we could do to improve their lot. We can realise that sometimes it is easier to do something than sit on the fence and regret that we did nothing for the betterment of society and for the betterment of ourselves.

It is sometimes so familiar for us to act as judge and jury. We can believe that we are experts on violence, on poverty, on how the whole world rotates. We can then even make cases to be the so-called independent, or intellectual voices and preach, to all who are interested our views on crime, education, marriage. Sometimes of course those peers whose opinions we value so highly are not even bothering to listen to us. Issues like land can be powerful weapons and we only have to look at the effects that the fight to keep the land have had on the world. The traditional tales of evictions from the land and ownership can turn to desperate debacles of humiliation, indignation and segregation. The real voices, the ones that deserve to be heard are the ones who strive to make changes, no matter what their circumstances are.

Some people don't seem capable of going forward and they continue to absorb and carry the mixed messages. They are fearful, lost and confused. This can be most obvious in men, who for years strived to disguise their feelings and their weaknesses, through an adopted persona of power and authority. This was their protection. But the message has changed, albeit slowly, and women now have more power and positions of responsibility. Some men who are frightened and unsure of this new found power are running fast and furious — but only from themselves. Ultimately we all have to look inside ourselves and see what we really are. We may not always like what we see and emotions may well be stirred, but on doing this we will be released from our own confusion and the conflicting messages that we have almost become immune to. Our initial unease will fade and we will have a new outlook.

The echoes of our forefathers may indeed still take time to leave our heads, but is it not time to take out the old tape, weary and tired and insert the fresh, new one? Language is the tool. Interpretation is the process. From the womb to the tomb we all deserve to be clear in our heads and to send ourselves clear messages that will strengthen, energise and leave us better prepared to for the cards that life deals us.

Children and teenagers learn by example and we must stop pretending that we are ever going to find Nirvana. We are never going to have everything that we want. The answer is accepting and wanting what we have. We seem to take much in our lives for granted, our health, our families, our friends, our talents, our work, our security. There are so many things in our lives that we are so lucky to have and we should constantly remind ourselves of this fact. We may sometimes have to connect with our child-like qualities and our sense of mystery to our adult selves. We can demystify the coldness and suppression around us and explore ourselves in an open and comfortable way.

We can ask questions. We can ask what is behind the mask, what is behind the answers that we are given, the answers to questions that we think may need more answers, the search for the truth. It is o.k. to ask questions, in fact it is positively necessary to ask questions. Loss of faith in ourselves leaves us with misplaced questions, misplaced answers and we can be lost in an ocean of uncertainty, with the heavy feeling that things are never going to change. However it is never too late to change, irrespective of what we might have done in the past. We can all move on. We can start to make sense of our hidden agendas, shadow selves, our fears, our scars, our secrets, our pains. our stigmas, our shadows, our labels. In essence we can rid ourselves of everything that has blocked us, aided our stumbling selves and prevented us from walking the road that will bring us freedom and peace of mind. We must learn to get to know the real self, the self that has struggled on when things were at the bleakest, the self that has coped in times of adversity, the self who has the fears, the hopes, the joys, the expectations, the questions and some of the answers.

All the different facets in our beings are part of us and we can take action. We can choose to take part rather than look on. We are responsible for our own happiness, our own choices and our own joys. We can nourish ourselves and give ourselves the permission to make mistakes and the permission to know that we can learn from them. We need to have compassion for ourselves, and of course for others and we need to connect with and detect the real messages. We need to know how to protect ourselves. We need to avoid subjecting ourselves and others to harmful, abusive or threatening behaviour. If you like and support yourself, respect others for who and what they are, enjoy the simple things in life, realise that you are unique and special and important. Well then you are free, you are home and dry. Communication with yourself and others can only get better when you unravel the mixed messages. Thank you for taking this message. Please keep in touch.